RHINO ROAD

Non-fiction books by the same author

CARPET SAHIB

(a biography of Jim Corbett)

THE TRIADS

(The Chinese Criminal Fraternity)

Martin Booth

RHINO ROAD

THE BLACK AND WHITE RHINOS OF AFRICA

Constable · London

First published in Great Britain 1992
by Constable and Company Limited
3 The Lanchesters, 162 Fulham Palace Road
London W6 9ER
Copyright © Martin Booth 1992
ISBN 0 09 471250 6
The right of Martin Booth to be identified as the author of this work
has been asserted by him in accordance
with the Copyright, Designs and Patents Act 1988
Set in Linotron Bembo by
Servis Filmsetting Limited, Manchester
Printed in Great Britain by
St Edmundsbury Press Limited
Bury St Edmunds, Suffolk

A CIP catalogue record for this book
is available from the British Library

for
RON THOMSON
who introduced me to *Ceratotherium simum*
and
CALVIN COTTAR
for a fly-camp in the Mara

Civilised man has spent untold treasure preserving ancient buildings and works of art fashioned by his own hand, yet he destroys creatures of ageless beauty. And he does so for no better reason than to boast of his prowess, achieved by means of a weapon designed by man to destroy man . . .

George Adamson

Contents

Illustrations

Acknowledgements

In the writing of this book I am indebted to the following: to W.R. (Ron) Thomson for many hours in the bush, walking, talking and stalking and to both him and his wife, Elza, for their generous hospitality in South Africa; to Calvin Cottar for his considerable help, advice and information, not to mention safaris; to Glenn and Pat Cottar for the loan of their private bush home on the Athi river and access to their family records; to the staff of Cottar Safari Service, Kenya for cold beers and long drives; to the anti-poaching staff of the South Luangwa National Park, Zambia for taking me on patrol with them; to Keith Harris and the staff of Lions of Longleat for the hands-on experience of Panzer, the white rhino bull; to Keith Markham MRCVS who rashly came into the bush with me and whose wildlife companionship I value greatly; and to my wife, Helen, for her considerable help in researching background material, checking proofs, making coffee, and for plucking up the courage to put her hand behind a rhino's leg.

M.B.

Preface

To write about the African rhinoceros is to relate an intense love affair that has held me in its thrall since boyhood.

Although I did not realise it then, I was immensely fortunate and privileged to live in Kenya for three and a half years, from 1956 to 1960, at a time when East Africa was still largely a wild place, unscarred by slash-and-burn farming, unbisected by tarmac highways, unpolluted by expanding cities or human populations, and unadulterated by the sisal and pineapple farms which today run in spiky regimentation to the very horizon. It was, perhaps, the last decade in which East Africa was still largely unsullied, with vast tracts of virgin veldt or forest.

One could not escape wildlife and all its wonders which impinged on my everyday life: although my family lived in the suburbs of Nairobi, wild creatures regularly visited us. Hyenas came punctually on Wednesday nights to knock over the dustbins before the Thursday morning garbage collection; leopards stalked (and occasionally ate) the neighbourhood pets, especially dogs; a cacophony of frogs (tree- and land-dwelling) punctuated the darkness in the rains; Bambi-like dik-dik[1]* and Thomson's gazelles[2] stepped daintily through the roses, nipping off the buds before dining on the vegetable patch; kokomonda lizards rustled through the leaf debris under the bushes and snakes glided through the grass. One night, I was awoken by three lions carousing in the ditch not ten metres from my bedroom window.

Surrounded as I was by the proximity of both big and small game, it was inevitable that I should become first curious, later fascinated and finally entranced by it. I drew portraits of the emerald-green and red-winged locusts with spines on their jumping legs as cruel as those of a cactus; I caught, chloroformed and pinned butterflies to setting boards; I tracked small game through the patches of bush near the house, lying in the grass to study passing

* Notes and References begin on p.203.

15

elephant shrews sprinting by on their little paths; I watched weaver birds crafting their nests and shrikes catching grasshoppers to impale on thorns. I kept 'tame' chameleons in my bedroom which served a dual purpose: firstly, they were unique and cosseted pets and, secondly, I was allergic to DDT and my resident reptiles ate all the insect intruders. There was, however, a disadvantage for Africans are superstitiously very afraid of chameleons and the servants predictably and justifiably refused to enter and therefore clean my room: that was left to me.

From time to time, with my parents, I visited a game park or drove out into the bush for a picnic. These were magical trips into the hinterland of the primeval, long before the crass invasion of zebra-painted minibuses and pink-fleshed tourists. Nonchalant lions came close to the car, zebras stamped at the mechanical intrusion, hippos snuffled in the rivers, crocodiles drifted easelessly beneath the overhanging boughs. Giraffes peered at the vehicle through long eyelashes, and uncountable numbers of buck continued to graze unheedingly. Vervet monkeys scampered in the grass and arrogant baboons sat on vehicles to bend or steal the windscreen wipers, hitch a ride or beg for scraps of food: later, by the end of the 1950s, these devious and intelligent primates had learned how to operate car door handles with some bad maulings of the occupants as a result.

On rare occasions, I encountered elephants, usually in the far distance. There were still vast herds of these magnificent creatures wandering East Africa but, for the best part, they kept away from dense human habitation and I made only sporadic forays into the real bush. When I did see them it was invariably through binoculars, grey humps moving through dense foliage or tall grass.

Only once during my teenage years in Kenya did I spot a wild rhino in the bush, although I did come upon a captured cow at the Carr-Hartleys' game ranch. This was contained in a pen of very stout tree trunks which had been embedded deeply in the earth, and which she desultorily charged – with little effect.

Yet there was that one occasion in the wild when I came face to face with a black rhino – the species indigenous to East Africa – and that brief span of three minutes or so has haunted me ever since and spawned an admiration and concern deeper than that I have ever felt for any human or man-made achievement.

16

This book, a personal one by the very nature of my relationship with wild animals, is born out of those few minutes – experienced over thirty years ago – and remaining as vivid to me now as they were then.

Martin Booth
Somerset 1992

— 1 —

RHINO ROAD

THAT first wild rhino appeared to me south-east of Mtito Andei on the main road from Nairobi to Mombasa, some-time in early August 1959, when my family was en route for a holiday on the shores of the Indian Ocean.

In those days, the road to the coast was unmetalled and ran in long straight sections transected every so often, once it had left the veldt grasslands, by steep drifts. These were valleys three hundred metres wide and up to fifty deep, filled at the bottom with loose rocks and treacherous sand or dank puddles and cloying potters' mud, depending upon the season. The lowest parts of these drifts were littered occasionally by skeletal vehicles caught by flash floods, always by rusting sump covers, silencers or exhaust pipes ripped off by the stones.

In the heat-bleached skies of the dry season – one did not attempt this road with a saloon car in the wet season unless it was utterly unavoidable – indolent vultures rode the invisible chimneys of thermals: all along the roadside was impenetrable grey-green thorn bush thickly coated in dust.

It was a monotonous journey. The only plentiful and obvious signs of wildlife a driver saw were piles of elephant droppings in the roadway: the creatures invariably dunged on the road out of fear at smelling men and machines. From time to time, in the far distance, one could see antelope standing in a liquid heat haze, but by the time one reached the spot where they had stood, they were long gone. The vultures overhead were waiting as much upon an incautious gazelle or zebra in the path of a speeding car or truck as they were a lion's kill.

In those latter years of the 1950s, there were no Toyotas or Nissans, no Range Rovers and certainly none of the huge trans-

19

African petrol tankers which now wend their ways to Burundi, Zaïre, Ethiopia or Sudan. Driving this road, one could spy another vehicle as infrequently as once in fifteen or twenty minutes. At their approach, windows and air vents were closed, headlights switched on. This was a wise precaution as the dust which issued from every oncoming vehicle could be thicker than the densest smoke. It blotted out the way ahead and seeped insidiously into even the most apparently airtight car. Headlights warned any second vehicle anticipating overtaking the first.

At intervals, there were signs of human settlement: there might be a straight path off into the bush that was clearly not made by hooves or paws but feet and bicycle wheels, or a pile of kindling left by the roadside, bound by thongs of leather or strips of rubber cut from lorry inner tubes. Nearing a settlement, people appeared on the road: a woman walking slowly in the heat with a bundle wrapped in brightly coloured cloth balanced upon her head, or a man lackadaisically pedalling a cumbersome black Raleigh cycle with a cargo of firewood, chickens or fodder strapped to the rear carrier. Sometimes, the cyclist would be carrying a passenger sitting side-saddle on the carrier, the pair weaving awkwardly to keep their balance and avoid the ruts and pot-holes. Nearer still, the bush would gradually become more open with small *bomas*, enclosures of cut thorn bush surrounding low, thatched mud huts. Herds of goats or native cattle would appear, guarded by *totos*, small children dressed in colourful rags who waved at the passing vehicles and flicked switches across the rumps of their charges to keep them from the road.

The little towns through which the road passed were nothing more than an agglomeration of mud huts, tin shacks and a few brick-built buildings which were Indian-owned *dukas*, general stores selling everything needed for subsistence, with a few extras which hinted of the wondrous life in Nairobi or on the coast 150 km. away in either direction. These consumer luxuries consisted of electric torches and Ever Ready batteries, pen-knives and razor-blades, toothbrushes and powder, Kiwi boot polish and aspirin.

And everywhere, there was the insidious dust. It changed colour according to the soil: ochreous orange for red murram, grey for black cotton, beige for sandy earths. It billowed out in impenetrable clouds to the rear of every vehicle. Passers-by muffled their faces as a vehicle approached, turning their heads away from the blast-wave of fine impervious grit and were instantly lost to sight in the fog as it rolled over them. If there was no breeze, it hung in the air for minutes.

I first travelled down that road at the age of thirteen, in 1957. For me, it was a long and tedious journey after the car bumped off the tarmac surface just a few miles south of Nairobi, hitting the murram. For an hour or so, we drove across the Athi Plain, rolling grass veldt scattered with thorn trees and invariably shimmering in a heat mirage in which stately antelopes walked slowly, as if bludgeoned by the heat. Zebras stood by the roadside and, on occasion, giraffe stared with a disinterested gaze upon the car. I watched these creatures with detachment as we sped by, much as any traveller might view what seems only transitory. After passing a few low rocky hills, the grassland gave way to scrubby bush and then, past the wayside inn of Hunter's Lodge at Kiboko, the dense cover began. The wide open views of the grasslands were gone and no animals – save those on the road ahead – were to be seen. The monotony, which would last almost to Mombasa, set in – or so it seemed.

Yet it was on this road that I saw my first wild rhino.

We were travelling in a two-tone grey Austin A55 saloon: my father was driving. At a petrol stop at Mtito Andei, another traveller coming inland from the coast warned us of elephants on the road near Voi but that was an hour's drive or more away.

The road drummed on, the car vibrating with both heat and impact with the ruts. Then we saw elephant droppings on the road.

As we rose out of a particularly steep and bone-jarring drift we saw, far ahead, a grey blob in the centre of the road, distorted by heat and dust.

'Elephant,' my father remarked tersely and he eased up on the accelerator.

Today, the unwritten (if seldom complied with) code of the road is that wild animals have the right of way, whilst in those days it was not so much the rule as a wise procedure to follow. Elephants were known not to balk at charging a vehicle, and even a small gazelle could crack a radiator or bend a mudguard, which could mean a long, hot, thirsty and even potentially dangerous wait in the bush for a breakdown service. Very few vehicles carried game fenders, unless they were off-the-road safari cars.

As we slowed, the cloud of dust we had been throwing up billowed forwards over us. We quickly wound the windows up,

21

holding our breath until the glass was snugly shut. Ahead, there was nothing to be seen but a dense red fog of talcum-fine murram. We cruised to a halt. My father could not see the pot-holes even a mere three metres in front of the bumper. He switched the engine off to prevent overheating, the ensuing silence almost oppressive. The insidious heat welled in through the roof, as if seeping osmotically through the steel. There was nothing to say and nothing to do until the dust had settled, so we sat and watched as it slowly disseminated.

Gradually, as the mist settled, a vague grey blur appeared in it about fifty metres distant. It looked solidly immovable even through the dust cloud. It did not move. The dust was caught by a breeze whipping along a game path and suddenly, it was dispelled. We wound open the windows. The grey blur materialised.

In the centre of the road stood a mature black rhino bull. He was side on to the car and was facing away from the vehicle as if he had turned away from the rolling dust cloud. His bulk seemed to block the entire carriageway.

Slowly, as if with an air of infinitely strained patience, he looked at the car, his head in profile. His front horn was long and thin, the second a distinct bump halfway up his nose. His tiny eye squinted at us. He gradually turned head on to us, his ears pricked. He twitched one of them as if adjusting the direction of their signal. He was no longer grey – that had been a misconception perhaps encouraged subconsciously by our expecting to encounter elephant – but a dull red. He had been dry-wallowing on the verge of the road where vehicles, passing over a tiny *donga*, a dried-up stream bed, had thrown up a miniature dune of soft sand and heavy dust.

It was a stalemate. He could not see us clearly with his inefficient eyes but he knew we were there. He could hear the clicking of the cooling exhaust pipe, the squeak of the suspension as one of us moved in the car: my father hissed for us to sit still. He could smell the hot oil, the baking metal, the tang of exhaust fumes but he could not discern the taint of humans. To wild animals, a vehicle is not a boxful of men and a threat, but a curiously shaped and coloured ant-hill, a rare and obnoxious cactus, a particularly unique patch of evil-smelling and inedible bush. If it does not move, or it shifts itself very slowly, then it is not a threat.

For a few minutes, rhino and Austin surveyed each other. It occurred to me that, the car being painted grey, the rhino might assume it was a foul-scented relative and might come closer for an introduction but it was not to be so readily fooled.

The rhino made not the slightest sound. Elephants often snorted at the proximity of vehicles, flapped their ears in a threat display, screeched or bellowed through their trunks: yet this vast animal made no display. It was as if he was quite self-assured, fully aware of his supposed impregnability. As we watched, an ox-pecker, also known as a tick-bird[1], landed on his rump but he paid the bird not the slightest attention. The only part of the rhino which moved was his ears.

Quite suddenly, with an exceptional agility, the rhino jinked his fore-quarters around, much as a frolicsome heifer bothered by horse-flies might, and with his head held higher as in a show of almost grandiose self-consciousness, he trotted briskly into the thick scrub. We waited another minute or two and then set off once more, driving very slowly past where the rhino had entered the cover.

I had expected to see a track through the bush such as a Sherman tank might have made. There was no sign of his point of entry save his footprints in the dust dune. No twig appeared to have been snapped, no branch misplaced.

'He's gone,' my father said. 'He'll be four hundred yards or more off by now.' He pushed down on the accelerator pedal and changed up a gear.

I looked over my shoulder, through the back window of the car, hoping to catch another glimpse of the rhino, but all I could see was the dust-cloud travelling with us once more.

From that day on, I called the main Nairobi-Mombasa highway Rhino Road, although I never saw another wild black rhino on it.

Yet an intense fascination with and love of these huge, supposedly cumbersome beasts was begun. That they appeared to be an ugly remnant from a time of prehistoric creatures did not occur to me. I regarded them then as I do now, as certainly unusual but nevertheless immensely handsome animals whose very survival depends entirely upon the actions of mankind, their only real natural enemy.

2

THE EVOLUTION OF RHINOS

R HINOCEROSES are prehistoric mammals which have survived into modern times, against all the odds of evolution and change, almost as if in defiance of the laws of natural progression and history.

They are classified as perissodactyls or 'odd-toed ungulates' and are descended from the first mammals to evolve hooves: they are therefore in the same group of animals as tapirs and horses. Their precursors were the paenungulates (almost-hooved ungulates) and the protungulates (first-hooved ungulates) of which no examples now exist. They came into being in the Eocene period about 50 million years ago, reaching the zenith of their occupancy upon earth about 35 million years ago. They are now largely superseded in evolutionary terms by the even-toed ungulates (the artiodactyls) which include gazelles, deer, antelopes, giraffes, camels, pigs and hippopotamuses.

Compared with rhinos, these creatures have evolved to a very advanced stage, with acute aural, visual and olfactory senses, the ability to move quickly – even the apparently cumbersome hippo can run at a good speed over land – highly developed brains and efficient teeth adapted to specific feeding patterns. They have also become ruminant, and are able to digest cellulose by bacterial action in the gut. This has ensured them a considerable natural diversity of shape, form and range of habitat, assuring them of a biological success that has eluded the relatively slow-moving and impercipient rhino.

By and large, the different species of rhino alive today remain very similar to those living hundreds of thousands of years ago. Their most immediate ancestor, the great Woolly Rhinoceros[1] survived well into prehistoric times, finally dying out as recently as the

Stone Age. Neolithic cave drawings at Rouffignac and Font-de-Gaume in the Dordogne region of southern France show them to have been much larger and considerably more hairy than their modern descendants, but otherwise they were the same, with long horns mounted on their noses, comparatively short and stocky legs, and an impressive bulk. Those first human artists also depicted them as having humped shoulders, rather like those of the modern white rhino, only of a more pronounced nature, and to have been worthy of the hunt.

At the beginning of their evolution, rhinos were much more like horses: these rhinos, the *Hyrachidae* and the *Hyracodontidae*, had three-toed feet with long equine legs, enabling them to run at speed. There were also smaller and more robust varieties of rhino (the *Amynodonts*) which were semi-aquatic and had sharp incisors which they used as a defensive weapon as well as to feed. None of these animals bore horns: indeed rhinos, at the height of their natural success, were similarly hornless. For weapons, they had tusks formed from the lower incisors, somewhat like those of a modern hippopotamus. Indeed, they resembled the modern hippo more than the modern rhino.

The largest of all the rhinos was *Indricotherium*, one of these tusked animals. Fossil remains show rhinos to have stood six metres tall at the shoulder and to have been over nine metres from snout to tail, including a two-metre long head. A browsing vegetarian, it was so large, it had the reach of a modern giraffe and could feed from the tops of trees where it experienced no other major natural competitor for food. This magnificent animal represented the apex of rhino evolution, and lived at a time when rhinos were established throughout the temperate and tropical zones of the world. It inhabited what is now Eastern Russia, Mongolia and northern China, and became extinct about 10 million years ago.

The first creatures which one would recognise as being the forerunner of a modern rhino evolved during the Oligocene period 30 million years ago in North America and Europe. These creatures, known as the *Caenopenes* and the *Aceratheres*, were rhino-shaped yet they still bore no horns, but they carried formidable tusks, as did the last mentioned species, as well as the *Paraceratherium*, another massive rhino with heavy tusks, fossils of which have been discovered in northern China. This was a browser and fossil remains show it to have had pronounced low crowned molars ideal for crushing branches. As the North American and European rhino of the Oligocene period moved towards extinction in the Pliocene period, they began to form small horns on their noses.

In the middle of the Oligocene period, the evolution of rhinos divided into two branches, those creatures with one horn and those with two. Of the former, two successors survive today, the forest-dwelling browsing Javan rhino and the grazing Indian rhino. As with all rhinos, the browser is considered to be the less evolutionarily advanced. Both now exist in only tiny populations within highly protected and managed areas: about fifty Javan rhinos remain in one location – the Udjung Kulon National Park in Indonesia – and about 1,600 Indian rhinos live in thirteen reserves in India, Nepal and Pakistan.

The two-horned rhinos gave rise to the other surviving species. One is the Sumatran rhino: this is a direct descendant of the Woolly Rhinoceros and is, alongside the other modern rhinos, comparatively very hairy. A forest-dwelling browser, it has survived almost unchanged since the Tertiary period and is the most primitive of all the surviving rhinoceroses. About 600 remain in isolated populations in Burma, Malaysia, Indonesia and Borneo. The other species are the black and white rhinoceroses of Africa.

The two-horned rhinos reached Africa about 10 million years ago, having split from the root stock of the Asian two-horned varieties, evolving eventually into the two strains of African rhino. Their feeding habits precluded the need for incisors which they gradually lost, thus also losing the tusks of their ancestors. At the same time, they developed their horns as defensive weapons and aids to feeding.

The black, having remained a browser, is generally considered to be the more primitive of the two, whilst the white is thought to have evolved from the black into a grazing animal about 5 million years ago. They are, however, still sufficiently similar as to cause a controversy as to whether or not they should be regarded as separate genera or as sub-species of the same creature.

Despite the awesome size and apparent invulnerability of the rhinos, these larger perissodactyls are reaching the end of their evolutionary span – with the exception of the horse which has made itself indispensable to mankind, and thus ensured its genetic future. They are dying out in a world which no longer suits them and which no longer contains a natural niche for them to inhabit. Like

26

latterday dinosaurs in evolutionary terms, they are gradually disappearing, inexorably plunging towards extinction in a process which is being accelerated by the hand of man.

Why so many species of rhino have died out is a matter of conjecture. Their size makes it unlikely that they have ever been severely predated upon. The most likely cause of their demise is that climate change has altered the vegetation of their habitats. Many of the primitive rhinos were browsers and the change of woodland and forest into savannah or steppe grasslands, brought about by the ebb and flow of successive ice ages, destroyed their main food supplies. Atmospheric changes may also have produced a climate unsuited to the rhinoceros, which now lives only in tropical regions and has always seemed to prefer warmer climes. Unless they could evolve into grazers, they had no other option than to go down the cul-de-sac of extinction.

As rhinos were one of the largest animals alive in the prehistoric landscape, and unless provoked were generally slow-moving, they were comparatively easy prey to early human hunters, and could have been brought down either by spears or, more likely, by being driven into camouflaged pits lined with sharpened stakes or over cliffs. Indeed, at St Brelade on Jersey, in the Channel Islands, the fossilised skull of a Woolly Rhinoceros has been found at the base of a cliff, with the remains of many other human prey animals which were so killed by Neanderthal hunters. Hunters in Africa and Asia employed pit traps into the present century, until the advent of high-powered rifles.

To the primeval hunter-gatherer, the rhino must have been a prized quarry. Each beast would have provided at least 1000 kgs of meat per carcass. It also provided a substantial hide which could have been split several times, and would have been very supple when tanned. It is quite possible that rhino skins were utilised as tent coverings, just as mammoth skins were used to roof simple bivouacs constructed of the creature's bones.

Although hunted from the earliest times, it is certainly not until within recorded history – and, more specifically, the last three centuries – that man has had any real impact upon rhino populations, severely reducing numbers by specifically killing them in large quantities and at a rate the slow-breeding rhino has been unable to replenish. However, the main threat is not from hunting but from land cultivation. Loss of habitat in recent centuries, vastly acceler-

27

ated in the last seventy-five years, has hastened the natural process that wiped out the ancient species. In addition, heavy illegal game poaching in the last twenty-five years has brought the African rhino population to dangerously low, perhaps irrecoverable levels.

The rhinos have, furthermore, failed to compete effectively with ruminants which are biologically highly successful, and have found themselves forced into a corner. There is no main predator which feeds upon rhinos. The adult rhino is more or less invulnerable, although lions and, more particularly, spotted hyenas do success-fully predate upon young, and can reduce numbers significantly within localised populations. This predation has long been known to be the main cause of rhino deaths: calves are taken by hyenas, and there are reports of hyenas hunting in packs attacking an adult rhino, eating it alive by biting into its hindquarters and ripping at its belly. The effects of this predation are more marked where rhinos are artificially restricted, such as in a game park or national reserve surrounded by alien habitats such as cultivated farmland or heavily populated human areas. Other predation is rare, although I have seen a photograph taken in Kenya just before the First World War by an American hunter, Max Fleischmann, of a rhino being dragged into the Tana river by a fully grown crocodile, and I have heard of a rhino calf being hunted and killed by Cape hunting dogs. However, I doubt if these are common occurrences.

The rhino is biologically redundant. It cannot compete with the artiodactyls; it has ceased to evolve at a sufficiently rapid rate; it has lost most of its natural range; and it suffers now, as never before, from predation by humans.

It is impossible to save the rhino from its eventual extinction. There is nothing that can be done to halt this natural process. All that we can do is conserve the species now, so that it might, in the course of time, die out in a natural and dignified fashion.

3

UNICORNS
AND OTHER MARVELS

A N old boy of Rugby School, William Cotton Oswell, was the model upon whom Thomas Hughes based the Brooke boys in his novel; *Tom Brown's Schooldays*. In real life, he was a larger-than-life hunter who was sent to Cape Province to recuperate from an illness contracted in India. Here, in 1844, he fell under the spell of Africa and became, in time, one of the most important figures in the opening up of central Africa.

When he first set eyes upon a rhino, his remark was that it looked like a creature from out of time. Dinosaurs were virtually unknown in Cotton Oswell's life – the triceratops, the 'rhino-horned' monster was not discovered until the 1880s by Marsh and Cope in the USA – and so his remark was particularly astute. The rhino looked like no other known animal on earth, with its huge bulk and its sharp horns placed not side by side on top of its head but one in front of the other on its nose. It was the animal of legend, the ugliest unicorn.

Such a comparison between the rhino and the unicorn is not so far-fetched as it might seem: not only is the horn unicorn-like but the mythical beast is always portrayed as a horse, and the horse is the closest living relative to the rhino. Perhaps, somewhere in antiquity, someone saw a rhino and observed physiological similarities. Whatever was the foundation of the unicorn story, it has existed in the folklore of Europe and Asia (but not the Americas) for thousands of years.

Well before the time of Christ, the unicorn was established as one of a pantheon of mythical beasts, the magical prowess of which was legendary and the existence of which was unswervingly accepted as the truth: that unicorns existed was incontrovertible. To the Hebrews it was recorded in the sacred writings of the Kethubim as re-em; to the Greeks, it was the *monoceros* and to the Romans the *unicornis*, the latter words meaning 'one-horned'.

According to the Book of Job, it was a super-creature of fabulous strength, rather like an ox, which men had learned to tame and use as a beast of the plough. That this fabled unicorn was based upon a rhinoceros seems extremely dubious: it is more likely to have been an ox, possibly a yak or a buffalo, most likely a bison of some sort. And yet in heraldry, from the earliest period of heraldic art, the unicorn was often portrayed as a rhinoceros or, at least, a rough look-alike animal identifiable as such. In the Middle Ages, it made its way into the national coat of arms of Great Britain as well as on to apothecaries' shelves where the powdered bones and horn were listed as 'alicorn' and said to be an antidote to every known poison, and a cure-all for impotence or barrenness.

It was afforded more powers than mere strength and medicinal properties. Leonardo da Vinci wrote that 'due to its immoderation and lack of restraint, and its ability to cast off its natural modesty and wildness, [the unicorn] has a predilection for young virgins: when so affected, it ignores all distrust for mankind, approaching young girls when they are seated and falls asleep in their laps. This is the fashion by which hunters capture it.'

The unicorn legend was not restricted to Europe and the Middle East. Just as the rhino had ranged throughout the Old World, so did the legendary stories. In China, where it was considered a symbol of family and filial unity, the unicorn was regarded as a variety of stag with one horn and a dragon's head: it also had a horny, shell-covered, armoured back like that of a turtle. Frequently, it was illustrated as having three horns, a carthorse's bushy tail and a face not too dissimilar to that of a hare yet lacking the tall ears. The only anatomical detail that was accurate, assuming that the beast was really modelled upon a garbled version of the rhino legend, was its three-toed feet, yet even these were slightly wrong, being drawn as sharply clawed rather than blunt-nailed. It became a favourite subject of Japanese painters and even the great Hokusai, normally so accurate and vibrant in his depictions of the natural world, produced a number of stilted portraits of it.

The early Greeks thought the unicorn was a variety of wild ass, covered in snow-white fur with a dark crimson head and a long, spiralled horn in the centre of its forehead. This first description of the wondrous creature, by a writer called Ctesias, also notes that the horn was a remedy against poison and epilepsy. Its supposedly equine form curiously but coincidentally harked back to earlier much larger ancestors of which science was yet to learn. A closer examination of Ctesias' description suggests that he never saw this creature and was describing a mixture of the Indian rhino, the notoriously ferocious onager (a wild ass from Persia), the 'heran' (a gazelle) in which species some deformed males occasionally develop only one horn and the Babylonian 'rimu,' or (in Hebrew) 're-em,' which was a large ox or buffalo.

As soon as fossils were first discovered, it was frequently assumed that mammoth tusks, which, as they were fossilised ivory, appeared fabulous, were unicorn horns and the substance was termed 'unicornum verum,' or unicorn's head horn. The veracity of the unicorn's existence – past and extant – was increased with every find and although many theologians dismissed the matter and either pooh-poohed it or relegated it to the ranks of conjecture, there were many other thinkers who believed firmly in the beast: da Vinci, Mercati, Leibniz, Gesner and von Guericke wrote of the creature. Even Linnæus, the first classifier of the natural world, included it in his listing as a 'fierce, reckless and uncontrollable' animal. With the discovery of the narwhal, the unicorn myth was given a huge credibility.

The narwhal is a whale with a pair of tusks, really a twisted tooth growing forwards from the upper jaw, of which the left-hand example can grow to three metres in length, whilst the right-hand stays short thus giving the creature a unicornish appearance. These were soon considered as 'alicorn' and worth, quite literally, a King's ransom: the emperor Charles V discharged a huge debt to the Margrave of Bayreuth with the payment of two narwhal tusks.

Not until the nineteenth century did zoologists begin to dismantle the unicorn myth, although the discovery made in the late nine-teenth century of fossilised giant prehistoric rhinoceroses, classified as *Elasmotherium*, did go some of the way towards reviving the concept. Today, however, the unicorn fallacy is regarded as a fairy story: sadly, however, for the rhino, the magical properties of the unicorn appear to live on in the minds of modern man in the continued belief throughout the Middle and Far East of the medicinal and magical value of the unique horn.

Despite the fabled creature's existence in ancient legend, the real rhino was certainly known to the Greeks and Romans. Both

Agatharcides and Strabo wrote about it in recognisable detail, and the Roman poet, Martial, wrote of its ability to 'toss bears into the stars': Pliny states that the rhino was the sworn enemy of the elephant which it attacked by gouging its horn into the soft under-belly of the larger animal. These accounts were most probably inspired by the writers having seen animal contests between rhinos and bears or elephants: exotic animal fights were frequently staged for public entertainment in Rome. That Pliny writes of a single horn suggests that he had not seen an African two-horned rhino, but an Indian one. And yet other contemporary sources clearly distinguish between the one-horned and two-horned varieties.

Throughout the Dark and early Middle Ages, the knowledge of the rhino was lost to Western Europe. What little was known of it was fogged by the unicorn story. Ironically, the first rhino of which Europeans heard after centuries of ignorance was a two-horned creature – but from Asia.

In 1292, Marco Polo stopped in Sumatra on his way back from his seven-year sojourn in the Far East. There he saw what he described as 'lion-horns, with feet like those of elephants but much smaller and resembling a buffalo in the manner of the distribution of their fur and they have two horns upon their heads with which they harm no one.' What he had seen was the rarest and most primitive of all, the Sumatran rhino. Needless to say, he equated this with the unicorn story and wrote, 'they are nasty creatures, always carrying their pig-like heads close to the ground. They like to wallow in mud and are not in the least way like the unicorn as referred to in our European stories. Can such an animal of this race be at ease in a virgin's lap? I will say just this – the creature is entirely different from that we fancied.'

Nothing more was heard of the Sumatran rhino until five and a half centuries later when two were captured, semi-tamed with domestic elephants and shipped back to England where they arrived in 1872 and were held in London Zoo.

The Chinese knew more of the rhinoceros than the Europeans or Arabs and had done so for centuries. The *Ts'ien-han-shu Annals*, compiled in the reign of the Emperor P'ing in the third century AD, states: 'In the time of the Emperor P'ing, Wang-mang, as he reformed the government, aspired to show the power of His Majesty. He sent valuable gifts to the Lord of Hwang-chi with a request that the Lord should despatch an ambassador to him bringing as tribute a live rhinoceros.' In due course, 'these emissaries from Hwang-chi, travelling from a distance of 30,000 *li*,' are reported to 'have brought as tribute a living rhinoceros.' Hwang-chi is thought to have been a kingdom in southern Malaysia or Indonesia, so the rhino was taken over a great distance, indicating its value. It is a sorry thought to consider that it was probably killed for its medicinal parts: such would have been the fate of many other exotic beasts transported to Chinese courts over the centuries, including pheasants, white stags, tigers, lions, leopards, elephants and the rhino's distant cousin, the banded tapir.

The first picture of a rhino to reach European eyes since classical times was that drawn by Albrecht Dürer who, in the early sixteenth century, carved a woodcut based upon a rough drawing possibly brought to him by a merchant. His sketch, now one of his most famous, is of an Indian rhino which appears to be armour-plated in much the way that knights' horses were protected in mediæval tournaments. It is of interest to note, however, that the Indian rhino was, until recent times, sometimes referred to as the 'armoured rhinoceros', although it is no more protected by its skin than any other rhino: the name comes from its appearance, the loose folds of skin suggesting overlapping plates. Dürer's rhino has a horn on its nose, another smaller one on its shoulder and it appears to be covered in horny excrescences: there is a degree of artistic licence in the depiction.

Some time before the publication of Dürer's woodblock, the first living rhino since classical times had reached Europe. In 1513, after the establishment of the Portuguese colony of Goa on the west coast of India, a rhino was sent to King Manuel the Great in Lisbon. Interestingly, it developed a large number of wart-like horny growths on its skin during the voyage from India, and it may have been these which influenced Dürer's drawing. Whatever might be the case, these were taken as normal on all rhinos and continued to be shown on drawings until the eighteenth century when, in 1711, the travel journals of the Huguenot trader and jeweller, Jean Chardin, were published.

Chardin had lived much of his adult life in Persia and India where he dealt in gemstones (especially diamonds), and held a number of diplomatic posts on behalf of the British, for which service he was knighted by Charles II. The rhino he drew in his volume had not been seen in India but at the Shah's royal court in Isfahan. It, too, was an Indian rhino.

Although the one-horned rhino was the accepted version of the animal in eighteenth-century Europe, the Arabs, who had been slave- and spice-trading along the coast of East Africa for well over a thousand years, knew of the two-horned African rhino. Drawings of these had existed in Arabic literature since the late twelfth or early thirteenth centuries. Western zoologists, however, did not believe it existed. First, it was double-horned; secondly, the nose was sharp (being the prehensile upper lip of the black rhino); thirdly, it was smooth and did not exhibit the folds of an Indian rhino's skin. Indeed, one museum curator who obtained a complete skin of the 'sharp-nosed rhinoceros' assumed that the creature had been under-nourished on its voyage and he ironed folds into the skin to make it appear genuine. It was only when other specimens arrived from Africa that the curator's error came to light.

Until the nineteenth century, no one assumed any rhino lived in Africa save the 'sharp-nosed' (black rhino) species which the Romans had referred to as an 'Ethiopian ox'. However, as trade with African coastal regions increased, very long rhino horns started to appear on the medicine market.

The Englishman, William Burchell – who discovered for science the zebra and a large number of other African animals, many of which bear his name to this day – had come upon a huge dead rhino in 1812, and taken drawings of its carcass. In 1817, he heard a rumour from Boer veldt-trekkers in South Africa of a living 'wijd rhino', said to be over six feet tall at the shoulder, two tons or more in weight and with one of its horns at least a yard long. Burchell translated 'wijd' as 'white' instead of 'wide' or 'big'.

Since Burchell's discovery of the last 'unknown' rhino, the animal has become not so much a subject of man's mythology as one of his greed and lust for blood. Even as early as 1900, a white hunter named Major Powell-Cotton brought one sub-species down to such an insignificant population that it is now near extinction. He was hunting in the region of the Upper Nile and shot a number of white rhinos in the border country of Zaïre, Sudan and Uganda. This shook the hunting, zoological, taxidermist and naturalist fraternities, which had assumed that the white rhino had never lived north of the Zambesi river system. Scores of hunters and others converged on the area over the next decade, including Theodore

Roosevelt, at the time just recently retired from the presidency of the USA. The animals which Powell-Cotton did not kill were soon being hunted down.

This animal was the last descendant of the giant rhinoceros which had lived since prehistoric times on the southern edge of the Sahara. It was, like all rhinos, on its inexorable way towards extinction, but the arrival of hunters speeded up the process by thousands of years.

This northern white rhino was accepted as a sub-group of the southern white rhino and was named Cotton's Rhinoceros.[1] A few creatures survived into the middle of the twentieth century; the first zoo ever to receive a pair into captivity was that in Antwerp where the animals arrived from Sudan in April 1950. It is now considered to be all but extinct in the wild. The myth nearly over.

— 4 —

MOTHER NATURE'S TANK

B Y weight, the rhino is the second largest land animal after the elephant, and has been for aeons. A fully grown black rhino may weigh as much as 1400 kgs whilst the larger white rhino may top 3600 kgs. That it resembles an animal tank, is bulky, solid-looking, formidable and appears utterly impregnable, goes without saying, but in truth the rhino is exceedingly vulnerable because of its size, the way it lives, and the loss of its specialised habitat, which is why it is nearing the end of its evolutionary viability.

The rhino is an ungulate and a herbivore, consuming only vegetable matter. It is therefore what is termed a primary consumer. It is one of those animals whose ecological vocation is essential to all of those animals higher up the food chain, as the prime mover in the process of cycling energy from plants into all other creatures up to carnivores. In other words, along with all the herbivores, the rhino's ultimate role is to convert plant material into flesh that might subsequently be eaten. At the same time it acts as one of nature's gardeners: by eating plants it encourages growth, disperses seeds, makes manure, and through its use of certain habitats protects them. In short, the herbivores pass on the basic energies of the earth through their bodies to those creatures unable to take it for themselves, be they the big predators (lions, tigers, leopards), small predators (foxes, cats) or the ultimate predator, man.

Today, the rhino, once it becomes a mature adult, is hardly preyed upon, and only rarely killed by a natural prey (excluding man). In prehistoric times, rhinos were most probably diet items of the very large predators, such as the sabre-toothed tiger, which are now extinct: fossilised bones of rhinos show teeth marks, although these may have been caused by scavenging rather than hunting.

Now the rhino is more or less secure from predation but, that aspect aside, it has most of the attributes and roles of other ungulates in the natural world.

Most ungulates are usually timid and quiet animals. If they carry weapons such as sharpened hooves, horns or antlers, these are invariably more for defence than attack, or as symbols of sexual prowess and ability to breed. They may be used to impress members of the opposite sex or threaten competitors in breeding or mating contests, but they are rarely offensively used unless to protect their young.

Being preyed upon, ungulates are invariably very well endowed with all the senses, and are suspicious and ever vigilant to any real or conceived threat. Their sight is usually very keen, their eyes positioned on the sides of the head to afford a maximum field of vision, the olfactory senses acute and their hearing highly attuned. Their most common response to threat is to run from it.

Except for its poor eyesight, the rhino is a typical ungulate in all these respects: it will even run from a threat if it can, or certainly avoid confrontation, despite its apparent invulnerability. However, on account of its size and solid construction, the rhino does not need to run fast as do, for example, other perissodactyls like the horse or zebra. Instead, the rhino has evolved a thick skin which can withstand the onslaught of even the largest modern predator.

This is not to say that it is immune to predator attack. Rhinos occasionally fight with lions and may lose, although their death is not caused by an outright killing, but comes to pass later from wounds incurred. Fights between rhinos and elephants have also been recorded with either or both dying from horn or tusk penetration.

The greatest enemy of the rhino does not, however, use claws and teeth: a well-crafted forged iron spear or a high velocity bullet can most effectively penetrate a rhino's hide.

Despite its bulk, a full-grown rhino can still be comparatively fleet of foot and can readily run or charge at up to fifty kms per hour. Under duress it can maintain this speed for the better part of a kilometre, sometimes more. It can walk without stopping for hours on end, even when wounded. What it lacks is the sustained speed of the other perissodactyls, although it does, almost miraculously it would seem, share their ability of turning quickly at speed. This is achieved not by fleet footwork but by allowing the momentum of

37

forward movement to swing the mass of the body round. When wanting to make a sharp turn, the rhino waits until a foreleg is outstretched to its maximum, then locks the foot still. The body turns around this leg as on a fixed point. In such a way, a rhino can move through up to eighty degrees without any significant loss of speed.

The build of a rhino is synonymous with ideas of strength. The legs are chunky and fairly short, the head is large, suggesting an ungainliness and inability to balance. It has the appearance of having been made by a committee rather than a single mind, a body built through compromise rather than considered blueprint. In fact, the rhino looks as it does because it is out of date. In its original world it would have looked more in place, more modish amongst the animal designs of its original contemporaries.

The spine is heavily constructed with the large vertebrae especially designed to carry the attachments of the heavy muscles which support the weight of the extensive intestines and comparatively large head. The latter, joined to the spine by surprisingly small atlas and axis bones, considering the mass of the skull, counterbalances the rest of the body, so that the centre of equilibrium of the whole rhino is over the front legs. The pelvic bones are vertical and at rough right angles to the spine to support the considerable weight of the hindquarters, the muscles of which are also the power-house for forward motion. Additionally, the rhino has more ribs than the other perissodactyls, again in order to lend added strength and support to the body.

The front legs carry the rhino's weight; the rear legs provide thrust for forward movement. Each foot bears three toes, unlike those of the artiodactyls which have two. Prehistoric rhinoceroses had four toes on their front feet, the third taking the weight. In modern rhinos, it is the middle toe which takes the weight of the body, rather than having it spread between the toes as occurs in the artiodactyls.

When a rhino walks, the movement of the front foot is interesting. As the leg lifts, the foot relaxes and appears to thin down to a uniform thickness along its whole length; then, as it touches the ground again and the weight of the body is taken, the toes splay outwards to form a pad of bone and muscle, distributing the weight. The foot becomes, in appearance, a little like that of a camel.

Many ungulates live in herds for, amongst other reasons, protection in numbers. Being fleet of foot they can confuse predators by stampeding. Being comparatively small consumers, they can afford to live in large groups. Being mobile, they can migrate with food supply and demand.

The rhino, on the other hand, is not sociable, and generally keeps away from large gatherings of its own kind. Its size makes group living for defence unnecessary and its digestive system and feeding behaviour are ill suited to a nomadic life. As it consumes comparatively large quantities of food, and is a selective feeder, so it is impracticable for it to feed in herds.

The rhino takes a long time to digest its food which must be present in large quantities. Its diet, being exclusively vegetarian, contains very large quantities of cellulose, and its method of dealing with this is different from that found in the artiodactyls. In the latter, specialised bacteria in the stomach break the cellulose down, but in the rhino this is done in the caecum, allowing the animal to eat heavily.

A rhino's teeth are unspecialised, which is surprising when one considers the specialisation found in other ungulates. This despecialisation has come about through an evolutionary process which began with distinct variations in dentition: the early rhinos, in addition to defensive tusks, had sharp incisors suited to both grazing short grass and browsing on shrubbery. The incisors were 'self-sharpening', having a vertical groove in them which let them remain keen as they were worn down. The African rhinos, being the more advanced of the five remaining types, no longer have incisors.

Those first rhinos were also endowed with low-crowned molars for grinding on leaves and twigs. In due course they evolved high-crowned molars suitable for grazing, extending their food variety and ensuring them an increased evolutionary lifespan. The age and identity of a rhino fossil are determined by the development of its molars.

Present-day rhinos eat a wide variety of food plants. The white and the black species differ in their choice of food, which allows them to occupy the same ranges, when populations are mixed and dense. This is almost certainly one reason for their survival. As climate and vegetation have changed, so they have been able to adapt and compete for food sources. It is equally certain that the

39

other extinct perissodactyls disappeared because they could not adapt to changing circumstances, nor could they compete with others of their kind for the dwindling supplies of their comparatively specialised diet plants.

As a result of the rhino's prodigious feeding, each animal has to maintain a territory under its sole ownership, in which it can feed more or less exclusively. Each rhino moves slowly around its specific area, to quite an ordered timetable or schedule, governed by seasonal plant growth. Other rhinos are excluded from its territory by infrequent formal 'battles'. Larger rhinos are invariably victorious over their smaller neighbours in these comings together. On occasion, however, other inferior rhinos are tolerated if present on the territory.

Although rhinos will compete aggressively for rights to feed in certain areas, water sources, especially where these are scarce, are usually communal. In areas where rhino populations are substantial, it is not uncommon to see three or four congregating at a water hole, mixing quite amicably with each other without any signs of competitive behaviour. I have seen nine rhinos at a water hole simultaneously, none taking the slightest bit of notice of the others. This intermingling is not restricted to one species at a time. In the Republic of South Africa, where both black and white rhino conservation is effective and very well organised with mixed populations co-existing in relatively small areas, both types of rhino will go to water together.

Access to water is essential to all rhinos and it is the availability of water and not food that determines the carrying capacity of an area. Most rhinos must drink daily, although during a drought or prolonged dry season, they can survive for three or four days without water.

Water is not required solely for drinking. As the rhino cannot sweat, it relies upon water and mud as cooling agents. Although it has a wide body temperature range, from 31°C to 50°C, the rhino can overheat, and does not have the advantage of the other very large mammal, the elephant. Both animals have tough hides which retain heat, but whereas the elephant has a cooling mechanism – it can keep cool by flapping its ears which are well supplied by blood vessels and which act as heat dissipators much like the vanes in a car radiator – the rhino has none.

Water is an excellent cooling agent, dropping temperatures

through evaporation: both elephants and rhinos bathe when they can, the former often playful in water. Mud is also an excellent way of dispersing heat. Under the hottest sun, it can take up to several hours to bake, taking heat from the body all the while. The mud not only cools the rhino but also provides other practical uses: it maintains the tough skin in a healthy and supple condition, vital to an animal which cannot groom. Furthermore, mud packs prevent bites from flies, especially the tsetse fly which can easily penetrate a rhino's hide, and the attention of other blood-sucking parasites such as ticks. Any ticks that are in place upon the skin when a mud wallow takes place are usually trapped in the mud and removed with it when it dries and flakes away.

The skin of a rhino is thick and tough, yet it is not so leathery nor as hard as that of the elephant. What is more, it is virtually bald by comparison, the elephant having coarse hairs over most of its body surface, sometimes the individual hairs being so wiry as to be made into long-lasting native jewellery such as bracelets. Rhinos have very short, sparse body hair, more like a stubble, save at the end of the tail where there is usually a single small tuft: mud wallowing may remove this meagre covering of stubble.

Even in the softer parts, an elephant's skin is hard, but a rhino's is surprisingly very soft and supple. I have pushed my hand into the foreleg 'armpit' of a white rhino bull. The skin there is warm, dry and as smoothly pliable at the skin of my own instep. Behind the ears, it is as resilient as the skin on the palm of my hand: beneath the overlapping folds of skin above the front legs it is also of the same quality of touch as high-grade pigskin leather.

Rhinos are comparatively short-sighted, their vision poor although it is not so bad as was once believed: their eyes are comparatively small, a disc a quarter of the thickness of a human eye. The eyelid carries long eyelashes. They can comprehend movement and detail quite close up but their eyesight beyond about thirty metres is considered to be limited to a recognition of shades which remain anonymous unless they move. It has been suggested that this trait has survived their evolution from forest animals, which do not have to rely upon eyesight in thick cover. Certainly, the black rhino which prefers to occupy dense thickets has little use for long-distance vision: the white rhino, on the other hand, which lives in comparatively open terrain does require to see further and, indeed, has marginally better eyesight than the black.

Although it is not yet proven, it is thought that the rhino has binocular rather than stereoscopic vision, in keeping with most herbivores. There is a school of thought that opines that the rhino can see stereoscopically. When looking at a rhino head-on, one can *just* see both eyes, so it may be possible that the rhino can look forward at the same time as looking to the sides: however, this forward vision coming close to the rim of the eye is assuredly vague. It is my opinion that the rhino generally has very poor direct forward vision and this is why, at close quarters, it will tilt or move its head slightly from side to side when observing something directly to the fore.

Whereas its eyesight is not good, a rhino's hearing is acute. The ears are very large and each can swivel through about 110 degrees and can act independently from the other, making directional location and all-round protection readily accomplished. A rhino, in common with many other wild animals, also has a wide range of sound recognition and is aware of what other creatures are 'saying'.

The rhino's olfactory sense is also astute and refined. This is hardly surprising, since its nasal cavity is nearly three times the volume of its brain, about 3.5 litres to 1.1 litres. Scenting and chemical markers are a very important part of every rhino's life. Smell is vital in detecting threat. The black rhino, living as it does in dense thickets where sound signals may be confused or camouflaged, relies especially on its sense of smell. As in a vast number of animals, however, scent is not restricted to defensive use. For the rhino, smell is also a means of communication with others of its kind, and patterns of behaviour have formed around this social application of spreading individual chemical markers.

Urine and dung are important disseminators of an individual's scent. Male rhinos spray urine upon bushes or bare patches of earth (ant- or termite-hills are frequently used) in short, sharp, very fine bursts as a part of the process of establishing, demarcating and retaining ownership over a territory: the male rhino's penis points backwards when not aroused, having become specifically adapted to the act. Only males spray and they will do this only within their own territory: etiquette dictates that a rhino passing through another's domain – en route to a communal water source, say – will not attempt to spray. This established protocol avoids unnecessary confrontation.

At other times, urine is also sprayed as a means of warning off intruders and may be further sprayed as an indication of concern or worry, a signal to a possible threat that it will not be tolerated much longer. This is particularly useful to the rhino in times of conflict, and urine-spraying often accompanies confrontations and is done as an act of dominance. The threat need not be from another rhino: I have watched white rhino spray urine into the air at my approach as a signal that I am reaching the threshold over which I might not proceed without risking attack.

The rhino does not dung at random. It uses specific midden sites placed around its territory where it deposits its droppings. The black rhino in particular spends some time kicking these around with its back legs or turning them over with his horn. There are two reasons for this behaviour: first, it implants the individual's scent on its own feet, allowing it to trail its identification as it walks, and, secondly, this kicking overpowers any previous visitor's scent, thus establishing territorial rights. Rhinos also make scratch-marks on the ground with their feet, further spreading their scent. The middens are frequently found on borders between two animals' ranges, and thus act not only as a warning of ownership but also as a means of keeping in touch. Interestingly, the black rhino makes less effort than the white to drive others from its feeding range, but the ritualistic making of middens, urine-spraying and scratch-marking are still conducted, urine-spraying being the predominant means of posting borders. The female sprays urine at midden sites when coming into season as a means of informing visiting males of her readiness for mating.

The dung of black and white rhinos varies greatly, which is not surprising when one considers their very different diets. The black rhino's dung is full of undigestible twigs, sticks and thorns and may be a reddish colour, due not to internal lacerations but to the sap and leaves of the Nthombothi tree for which it has a distinct liking. A white rhino's dung, on the other hand, is green and steaming, and whereas the black rhino's dung remains bound together by the matrix of twigs, the white rhino's soon changes colour and dries to chaff.

Many creatures utilise and even depend upon the rhino's dung, especially insects. For instance, dung beetles use it to lay their eggs in and raise their larvæ, and harvester termites use undigested grass from it. It follows that insectivorous animals also use rhino middens, especially as these, being often large and dense, act as a

43

concentration for food. Banded mongoose, francolins, rollers, guinea fowl and the shrike,[1] all feed here: the latter frequently dust-bathes in dried dung, 'anting' as do jays. Small lizards also visit middens to feed, as do even larger reptiles such as monitor lizards. I have also seen the spoor of ant-eaters at large midden sites.

Also important as markers are dried pieces of skin rubbed off on trees used as scratching posts, or dropped in dried mud which has flaked from the animal after wallowing.

These keen sensory abilities are, of course, inherited from those times when the rhino was preyed upon as a diet item. Today, they are used most often in the rhino's social life or to detect the approach of men: I have heard tell of rhinos surviving in populations that have been heavily poached by native hunters, which have learnt to tell the difference between an African gathering honey or collecting firewood, say, from one armed with a powerful rifle. It has been suggested that the rhinos have become conditioned to the smell of gun-lubricating oil. Whether there is any truth in this assumption or not, one cannot be sure: I am inclined to doubt it, but it does show the almost supernatural sensory perception for which rhinos are sometimes given credit.

Mythical fairy stories about the rhino are legion. Apart from the supposed magical medicinal properties of its horn, there are many native folk tales. A well-known Zambian bush tale is typical of these and is relevant to the creature's dunging behaviour.

The story goes like this: once upon a time, when God made the animals, he asked them all to construct their own skins. To enable them to do this, he gave them each a needle, which every animal – save the dextrous monkey – accepted with his teeth. The rhino, however, being large and clumsy and forgetful and not very adroit, lost its needle and had to make do with a thorn. The result of this was that its skin was badly made and loose fitting. Furthermore, the rhino was afraid that it might have swallowed the needle and this is why it spends so much of its time after defecating kicking its dung about: it is still, after all these years, looking for the needle so that it can finally make a good job of its hide.

Hunters' and game wardens' stories are as innumerable as native ones when it comes to illustrating the behavioural or sensory abilities of rhinos. My favourite story was related to me by Ron Thomson, a noted game warden and considered to be *the* most knowledgeable authority on African rhinos: it was he who refined the rhino dart gun for use in his translocation programme when working for the game department of Zimbabwe, then Southern Rhodesia.

He tells of a black rhino upon which he came quite suddenly. Face to face with the creature at a distance of ten feet or so, Thomson stood stock still. The rhino could smell his presence but it could not see him clearly, even though they were so close to each other: being in front of the animal, he was not readily observable, suggesting – as I have mentioned above – that the rhino's forward vision is very poor. If he moved, it would hear him. Quite often rhinos rely upon two out of three sensory cues before they take action. Thomson could not move silently: the ground was thickly covered with dry dead leaves which he described as being like 'walking on corn-flakes'. For fifteen minutes, Thomson froze as if made of stone whilst the rhino remained standing before him patiently awaiting developments. It was a stalemate.

Somehow, Thomson had to convince the rhino he was not what he seemed to be. Very gradually, and being an adept naturalist capable of imitating animal sounds, he started to make the noise of a banded mongoose. After some minutes of this subterfuge, the rhino was convinced. Two cues were satisfied: the rhino identified an animal scent and related it to the sound of a mongoose. After being satisfied, the rhino turned and sauntered off and Thomson, sweating profusely, waited until it was safe and made his retreat with every muscle aching.

This story does more than indicate the poor quality of a rhino's eyesight and the perspicacity of its other senses. It also shows, contrary to all the ripping yarns of African travellers, hunters and tourists, that the rhino is at heart a peaceable and benign creature and not a confrontational beast such as has often been portrayed.

The rhino's fame and the cause of its downfall in recent decades at the hand of man are due to its horn.

In actual fact, it is not a horn in the sense that, for example, a deer antler is, for it does not have a bony centre. It is more like hair, being made of hollow fibrous tubes of keratin, about a third of a millimetre in width. The fibres are surprisingly loosely bonded together, which causes the horn to fray with age and use. African rhinos, which have sharp horns – especially the foremost of the pair of horns – actually sharpen these from time to time by rubbing them against trees and boulders: some are worn away in time by continual attention.

45

The foundation of the horn is a rough protuberance of bone on the front of the skull but the actual horn carries no nerve tissue or blood supply. It is not living tissue such as a cow's horn, but it will if lost regenerate slowly in mature animals and quite rapidly in youngsters.

In an infant rhino, the horn first starts early in life as a small red spot which seems to give the animal a degree of discomfort, for it will rub this against the ground or on a branch. At the age of twelve months, the primary (or anterior) horn is about 5 cms long and steadily grows thereafter to whatever length it may in the individual. The secondary (or posterior) horn usually grows at a slower rate.

The rhino's horn is a formidable weapon. The muscles of the neck are so powerful that a single thrust of the horn can easily impale a large adversary: records exist of white rhinos, possessors of the largest front horn which can grow to quite remarkable lengths – 200 cms has been recorded – killing lion by lancing completely through them. It follows, therefore, that a rhino can be a danger to its fellows and, in common with many creatures it has therefore developed a ritual form of conflict to avoid injury whenever possible. This is not to say that rhinos do not actually fight: indeed they do, and those who have witnessed a real battle have been awed by it.

When rhinos fight they run at each other, aiming their horns at their opponent's neck and forelegs. They also ram each other, either head or side on, the horn being used not only as a piercing tool but also as a hard instrument of contact. Such a blunt strike can do considerable internal damage, causing severe haemorrhaging: this is not to say that piercing does not occur and many are wounded, sometimes killed, by such injuries. The fight continues unabated, with a cacophony of sounds, until one of the combatants runs away. Should a fighter fall, the other will rush in and kill it by goring and then by trampling or kicking.

However, it must be said that such full-scale fighting is thought to be rare in the life of any rhino.

The most common cause of conflict – as opposed to combat – arises over territorial disputes between males and the ritual is fascinating to observe. The protagonists first stand face to face, perhaps only inches apart, and are immobile for sometimes up to fifteen minutes. During this time they assess each other's strength.

46

They then back slowly away from each other and rub their horns on the ground, perhaps to draw each other's attention to the size of the other's weapon. This completed, they go their separate ways.

Two other ritual confrontations are those known as head-flagging and strutting. Whilst still some way apart, male opponents stand facing each other, swinging their heads from side to side: this is frequently a precursor to the face-to-face stand-off and may be an act of boastful warning, displaying the size of the horns and the head. Strutting is also conducted at a distance. The males become stiff-legged and move with a jaunty, upright – almost bouncing – jerking walk. Quite often, they will leave the scene of a confrontation in exactly the same, seemingly devil-may-care attitude.

When a real battle does occur – or, more likely, when the rhino attacks an enemy rather than another of its own kind – the rhino withdraws some distance then charges with head lowered. It can accelerate to its top speed in about fifty metres. When it comes in contact with the enemy, it rams the front horn in and then flicks the head upwards and to one side. Small objects (like a man) are tossed over the shoulder: larger adversaries are disembowelled, the horn ripping sideways through the flesh. When the tossing is completed, the rhino will then attempt either to gore its victim on the ground or trample it. The rhino may also seek to strike sideways blows with its heavy head, banging the front against the victim.

The damage the horn can inflict is astounding. Once, on Rhino Road, I came upon the remains of a large car which had been attacked by a black rhino bull. The animal had apparently charged the vehicle side on, slamming its horn under the skirting board. The floor panel of the car was pierced to the full length of the horn and the outrider chassis member was badly bent. The bony base upon which the horn is mounted gives the rhino a very solid foundation upon which to ram its enemy and the brunt of the shock is taken by the front of the skull and the nose, where the bone is very thick, so there is no risk of damage to the brain. The car from which I saw my first black rhino was itself written off by a rhino on the same road, some months after my father sold it. The side blow from a rhino's head can also inflict considerable damage, stoving in vehicle body panels or utterly crushing the limbs of a man.

The horn does not only serve as a weapon *in extremis*.

During feeding, rhinos use their horns as implements. Water may be dug for with it and salt-rich earth loosened for consumption. Black rhinos are also known to hook down tall saplings so that they can reach the higher, more succulent, new growth, and mothers will frequently so pull down branches for their young. Females also use their horns for helping infants get to their feet. Both black and white rhinos will, in times of hardship, dig with their horns for grass roots, tubers and the like to eat.

The horn is, therefore, a symbol to other rhinos of its owner's dominance, power, genetic prowess and breeding status and serves as a warning. It is also a tool. For the black rhino, it has an amatory application too, for the animal uses its horn in courtship ritual, rubbing horns with its chosen partner: the male has also been observed rubbing the female's hindquarters with his horn prior to mounting.

Courtship, mating and breeding in African rhinos vary between the black and the white, but there are general similarities.

Births are most usually of a single young (a calf), with double births known but very rare. The female (cow) is able to give birth every twenty to twenty-two months and, in captivity under a controlled breeding programme, this rate is achieved but, in the wild, rhinos usually drop their young every three or four years. The male (bull) takes no part in the rearing of his offspring and does not stay with the cow any longer than it takes to court and mate with her: the males do not maintain a monogamous relationship.

Once born, after a gestation period which may vary from between fourteen to eighteen months (usually closer to fifteen in the black – the exact period is unknown – and sixteen months in the white, the calf stays close to the mother. When on the move, in the case of black rhinos, the calf follows its parent, whilst in the white it precedes it: this permits the black rhino mother, which lives in dense cover, to make a way for its calf through thickets, whilst the white, living on more open land, may keep an eye on its young.

The calves of both rhinos have their senses even more acutely attuned to potential danger than those of their parents and, quite frequently, the calf will raise the alarm to a threat as yet unrecognised by the mother. Certainly, calves have keener eyesight than their dams but this deteriorates with time.

The calf continues to be suckled for up to eighteen months but can eat solid food at three months. After weaning, it remains in its mother's company until the next infant is born, at which time the mother drives her penultimate offspring away. It will then either form a loose association with another of roughly its own age or join a childless female and behave as her offspring until such a time as she bears a calf of her own. It is not until sexual maturity is reached at about six years of age that the rhino becomes completely solitary.

It is often thought that the rhino is a silent creature with no powers of vocalisation. This is not true. Being generally a solitary beast or, in the case of the white rhino living only in very small groups, it has no need of a wide range of communicative sounds. It does not require to warn its fellows of approaching danger. However, the rhino does maintain a range of expressive sounds. When sleeping it frequently snores. If angry or frightened it will make an extraordinary whistling sound like steam escaping from a valve. At times of distress, it will make a most heart-rending sound which begins as a low moan and quickly rises to a whimpering, high-pitched pig-like squeaking squeal. Before or during a charge or mock-charge, it will huff, puff, snort and grunt and it can, in a fight against another rhino, give off high-pitched pig-like squeals. Females call to infants with a sort of miaowing sound which the infant reciprocates. When worried or distressed, infants whimper or mew.

The rhino is the Sherman tank of the animal kingdom. It is large, it looks ungainly, and when at rest it appears innocuous. Yet it has hidden depths and it can charge at speed and wreak havoc if it so desires – which it rarely does.

And the tank allusion is not misplaced: the black rhino makes regular tracks through dense cover, especially in the direction of water sources and these are frequently used by other creatures to go to water. Even man uses them. The rhino tank therefore is not merely a cumbersome if fascinating animal vehicle but also a path-finder, nature's bulldozer and grader which opens up thick bush so that other creatures might colonise it. The rhino is, in short, an important member of the ecological community.

– 5 –

THE BLACK RHINO

THE names of African rhinos are misleading: the black rhino is not black and the white rhino is not white. They are both naturally dull grey in colour, of rather similar hue to that of an elephant.

Ask the man in the street to name the varieties of rhino, and the African black rhino is the one most people know today. This was not always the case: the first rhino to arrive in a European zoo, as opposed to being imported by the Romans for their gladiatorial sports, was an Indian rhino which was bought by London Zoo in 1834, from a Major Farquhar, for the then princely sum of £1050: it survived for fifteen years and was known as the Indian one-horned rhinoceros. The first African rhino to arrive in the Old World was a female black rhino, purchased by London Zoo in 1868 for £1000: it was then commonly known as the two-horned rhino.

The black rhino[1] (as opposed to the white rhino) is so called by default. How this misnomer came about is the subject of a number of stories: some state that the name derives from the colour of the mud in which the first animals were found caked, whilst another suggests that the early Boer settlers named it white after the white men (other Europeans) whom they despised because they were timid: the black rhino was fierce and brave like the black men.

It is now generally accepted, however, that it received its name from the corruption of the Afrikaans word *weit* (Burchell, it will be remembered, spelt it as *wijd*), meaning big or wide. And certainly, the white rhino is the bulkier and wider of the two species: yet in fact the description refers not to the size of its build but to the shape of its mouth. In this lies the main difference between the two: the black rhino has a pointed prehensile upper lip which is thinner than the white rhino's upper lip which is square and comparatively wide.

The black rhino is also known as the 'prehensile-lipped rhino' and the 'browsing rhino'. A hundred years ago, it was believed that the name 'black rhino' actually covered two species, the two-horned black rhino and the blue rhino[2], the differentiation being the length of their primary (or anterior) horns. Perhaps the greatest of the nineteenth-century African hunters, Frederick Courtenay Selous – who had shot vast numbers of rhino for sport – finally argued against this division, his theory being proven correct in time. Horn size is dependent upon habitat and it seems to be the case that the drier the area then the smaller the horn.

Very rarely, the black rhino has *three* horns. I have not seen such an animal but they have been recorded with a third very small horn situated behind the secondary one. A three-horned black rhino was shot in northern Uganda in the 1930s, and there was said at the time to be a three-horned strain living in Northern Rhodesia but this has since died out. There has never been a one-horned African rhino, despite the following claim by the American explorer Osa Johnson[3]:

[The rhino] shook all over, his eyes bulged and then, as if to contradict these apparent evidences of fear, his jaw stuck out with a degree of determination that was almost comical.

'Keep grinding [*the camera crank*],' he whispered hoarsely back at me. 'This is a rare, one-horned specimen!'

After shooting the animal with a rifle, wounding it to make it charge the camera and stampeding a large herd of buffalo, the writer continues with a mixture of *naïveté* and callousness:

We had forgotten all about the wounded rhino until some of the boys gathering firewood found him dead. We sent Jepanda to get his hide and single-horned head, but found that instead of being a rare specimen, he was nothing but an ordinary rhino that some-how had lost one of his two horns.

Fortunately, such behaviour and attitude was rare amongst real white hunters.

An adult black rhino, the smaller of the two species, is about 3.5 metres long and between 1.5 and 1.9 metres tall at the shoulder. The

51

front horn in a mature adult averages about 1 metre in length and the rear horn up to 50 cms. The animal weighs around 1300 kilograms. The black rhino reaches sexual maturity at about five or six years old, and the female remains fertile for about thirty years, during which time she is capable of giving birth to between nine and fifteen calves. The natural lifespan of a black rhino in the wild is about forty years.

Originally, the black rhino was to be found in vast numbers throughout west Africa, Nigeria, southern Chad, the Central African Republic, the southern Sudan, southern Ethiopia and Somalia right through eastern Africa as far west as Zaïre and throughout the countries of southern Africa right to the Cape of Good Hope. By a century ago, its habitat had been reduced to about half that area, the animal having been wiped out of West Africa and most of South Africa south of the Zambezi river. This early reduction noticeably coincides with the opening up of those areas by white men. Not only was the animal prodigiously hunted for sport, killed for meat and eradicated to protect crops, but it was also driven to localised extinction by the destruction of its habitat which was beginning to be opened up for ranch-style farming.

Even the most ardent of hunters were shocked by the reduction in numbers of both rhino species: Selous was horrified in 1881 to discover that the black rhino was no longer to be found anywhere in western South Africa, having been shot out primarily by Boer settlers. Only fifty years before, sightings were still being made in Cape Province, the first part of South Africa to become colonised by other than local tribesfolk. By 1910, the rhino had disappeared completely from its western African range and Zaïre and was absent from most of Chad, the Central African Republic, Ethiopia and Somalia.

Today, the black rhino is to be found only in diverse pockets of population, all of them under considerable pressure from game-poaching, agricultural encroachment and habitat destruction, the reduction of water tables (brought on by human demand and land drainage for crop irrigation) and, in some places, tourism. The largest populations are to be found in Tanzania, Zimbabwe and the Republic of South Africa where zealous game protection programmes exist and anti-poaching control is efficient and effective, often to the point of ruthlessness. The second largest populations reside in Kenya and Zambia. In the former, stringent measures are

being made against poaching and habitat conservation is well organised and controlled. In the latter, poaching and habitat destruction,
particularly of the slash-and-burn subsistence farming type, are rife,
and numbers are steadily and consistently falling.

The world population of black rhino is hard to assess accurately,
but it is probably about 7000 animals. It is even more difficult to
estimate how many black rhino were alive fifty years ago, but a
conservative estimate of 150,000 animals would not be ill-judged.
Before 1800, the start of modern agricultural progress and the white
man's arrival in Africa, the total would almost certainly have been
in excess of 500,000.

Being a browsing feeder, the black rhino prefers to live in dry
scrub thickets and dense bush, as a general rule spurning the open
grasslands: however, it can be found in veldt, although usually close
to wooded areas or ravines with adequate cover. It may also be
discovered in forest up to an altitude of 3500 metres.

The prehensile upper lip, which is pointed into a kind of mini-
trunk of flexible muscle, allows it to grasp twigs and branches,
holding these in to its mouth. It is also used to push food into the
mouth like a finger. (I have heard of a tame baby rhino being able to
open cupboard doors with its pointed upper lip.)

The black rhino primarily feeds on the foliage of bushes, including leaves, twiglets, buds and shoots, and browses upon a wide
variety of Acacia with their long and needle-like spines, Dombeya,
Solanum and Euphorbia. This latter plant contains a copious,
sticky, milky sap and rhinos particularly favour it in the dry season
when it makes up for the shortage of water: all rhinos, in common
with many other African animals such as the oryx and the gerenuk[4]
have a knowledge of water-retaining plants. They will also feed on
coffee, tea and cotton bushes – and maize plants – thus making
enemies for themselves of both native subsistence and commercial
farmers: they will even consume rose and other ornamental bushes
if given the opportunity and can therefore be a pest to gardeners.

In order to browse from trees of a substantial size, the rhino is
known to stand upright against the trunk using its front horn to
lever branches downwards. It will also break down boughs with its
horn to browse on them on the ground. Away from cover, it will
feed on the seedlings of diet plants, long grass that it can grasp with
its lip and the fruits of a number of trees. It may also eat clover and,
if other herbivores have over-utilised or stripped the local environ-

ment, it will consume the dung of wildebeest[5], topi[6] and hartebeest[7].

The black rhino's menu is varied with over 200 species of plant being known to be favoured, some of them highly poisonous to other mammals. This specialisation of immunity has ensured the rhino a food source that is unique to its own kind and to some extent affords it a guaranteed minimum intake. In certain months of the year, the rhino particularly favours leguminous plants and if these are absent it will consume the droppings of gazelle, giraffe and even elephant in order to rectify the deficiency. After the rains, the black rhino may temporarily graze upon succulent new grass. It does not strip bark from trees as do elephants, nor does it gouge out pith and heartwood with its horn as the elephant does with its tusks. The rhino is, therefore, not a destructive over-utiliser of its habitat. In addition to vegetable matter, the rhino also eats naturally occurring salt or saline earth which it excavates either by digging with its front horn or by kicking with its fore feet. At places where salt is very plentiful, these excavations may be quite considerable and there exist in Kenya two known caves entirely worked by black rhinos: one is in the Aberdare Highlands and the other, large enough to accommodate several rhinos at once, is near Marsabit. In this, the roof is scored as if by a team of men with pick-axes but the marks were made by rhinos. Sadly, the rhino has been shot out now by poachers in both regions so these caves are no longer visited and utilised by their rightful owners.

An individual black rhino's home feeding range varies in size according to the season and the abundance of food. The carrying capacity of the land – the saturation point over which it becomes too crowded to support its inhabitants – decides the population. The animal can have a range as small as a dozen hectares but it may also have a territory of some square kilometres in size. In semi-desert areas where water and foliage are sparse, a single black rhino can occupy a range of 75 square kilometres. With the heavy reduction in rhino numbers in recent years, many animals have extended their ranges, no longer having any competition from other rhinos to face for feeding. Within its territory, the individual black rhino wanders about with regularity, feeding from specific plants at different times of the year, visiting these plants on a twelve-monthly cycle.

Feeding occurs naturally in the early morning and late evening, as is commonplace amongst most of the African herbivores: the heat of the day is too intense to allow for too much activity. Where black rhino populations have come under threat from human encroachment, however, a pattern of nocturnal feeding (and drinking) has been seen to develop. The black rhino can afford to feed at night: most of the other herbivores cannot allow themselves such luxury as the hours of darkness for them are times of vigilance against such nocturnal predators as leopards. The black rhino, having no such predators, is not affected – native rhino poachers are not equipped with infra-red night-sights on their weapons so the rhino is safe. It has been noticed that, once human predation ceases, the black rhino quickly returns to a diurnal feeding and drinking pattern.

During the rains, the black rhino may wander more widely than its territory. This may be a time of the year in which some flux occurs in rhino society and there is a re-aligning of territories and boundaries. The heavy rains may aid this by diluting territorial scent-marking sites – middens, urine-sprayed bushes and so on – and making each individual think that there are fewer of his kind in the vicinity.

Generally speaking, the black rhino must drink at least once every twenty-four hours but it may, in times of drought, drink only every two or three days: in the dry season, in common with elephants, it will dig for water with its front legs in dried up river beds or at water holes, going down as far as one and a half metres in its search, excavating a sloping, ramped hole. Furthermore, in the dry season, the rhino seldom moves more than seven or eight kms from water at the most, many preferring to stay within five kms. This not only concentrates populations around rivers and water holes, increasing the chance of meetings and ritual confrontations, but it also leads in times of severe drought to large numbers dying of thirst. Indeed, death by drought has, from time to time, been a severe scourge of rhino populations: in Kenya, in the mid-1950s, hundreds of black rhinos died of thirst in the Tsavo National Park, bull rhinos seeming to survive more easily than cows.

As the rhinos regard water as a common right to all, access is allowed to it. Black rhinos frequently approach water sources along well-defined pathways which can be worn under the animals' weight to a depth of twenty-five cms: these paths serve not only as highways to water for many various thirsty creatures but also inform other rhinos through whose territory the path crosses of the intention of the visitor. If he is on the path he is not looking for food and therefore extra energy is not expended on mock battles and stand-offs.

The black rhino, being unable to sweat, regularly wallows in mud, on average about three times a week when mud is plentiful. As has been mentioned, the water content of the mud lowers body temperature. The mud also removes parasites and provides protection against stinging flies and ticks: it also acts as a kind of cosmetic mud-pack and keeps the skin under the folds above the shoulders and around the neck supple.

In addition to wallowing, the black rhino frequently sand bathes, either in dried river beds, dusty bush clearings or in the ash of bush fires. This activity also helps to keep the skin in condition and abrasively removes parasites.

There are other parts of its body however to which the black rhino cannot pay proper attention, the area around the 'elbow' of the front legs being the main one. Here rhinos (both black and white) are frequently seen in the wild with open and weeping sores. Around these wounds the skin is dried and cracked, the tissue often pus-filled and infected by a filariform worm[8], which is passed to the animal by flies which infest the dung middens.

Many insects are also found on rhinos. Stomoxys flies are attracted to the blood issuing from wounds and I have seen bees apparently drinking from the tears that may weep from a rhino's eyes. Some rhinos are also infected by the larvæ of the Gyrostygma fly which may be found under the base of the horn where the insect lays its eggs: such an infection causes irritation and results in the rhino frequently scratching its horn on the ground or against trees.

Rhinos are also fed upon by more than twenty varieties of ticks some of which are exclusive[9] to the rhino. These parasites are, in turn, preyed upon by a variety of tick-birds, commonly known as ox-peckers, which also feed from other animals including giraffe, elephant and buffalo. They consume not only ticks but also mites from the rhino's ears.

Although through this symbiosis they give the rhino a positive service in parasitical control, tick-birds also annoy the rhinos by picking grubs from their nostrils and pecking at open wounds, causing increased infection. There is, however, another benefit the rhino derives from them: the tick-birds stand sentry duty on the rhino's back. At the approach of predators, including man, the birds take to the wind with a raucous, starling-like chattering alarm call which alerts the rhino to the proximity and direction of possible danger. The rhino can differentiate between the calls. The chattering alarm at a man's approach draws a rhino's attention, but the hissing kriss-kriss or tzik-tzik that announces the arrival of baboons is ignored.

Parasites are not removed exclusively by tick-birds. Turtles have been seen eating ticks from bathing rhinos: I have seen small white cattle egrets[10] riding on the backs of browsing rhinos similarly feeding from them.

Not all the rhino's parasites are external. Internally, rhinos are invariably infested with tapeworm, of which several varieties are commonly found in them, as well as other parasites such as the larvae of bot-flies which inhabit the stomach. The bot fly is a very large insect with a wingspan of about six cms. It is dark brown with reddish-brown legs, and although it mimics the pompilid wasp it has in fact no sting or any other defence mechanism. The insect lays its eggs on the skin behind the rhino's ears and on the neck; the larvae eventually work their way into their host to gather in the stomach where they hook themselves to the stomach lining. Eventually, they are evacuated with the dung, pupate in the middens and hatch as adults. The rhino is also infested with an assortment of flukes.

Like many wild animals, the black rhino sleeps in deep shade during the hot hours of the day. It may frequently be found sleeping standing up which affords the animal a quick escape if danger threatens. A rhino is clumsy in getting to its feet from a prone position and so resting 'on the hoof' is common. At times, however, rhinos may rest leaning against a tree or boulder. The black rhino does not necessarily sleep at night, especially if it is feeding nocturnally.

In areas where rhinos are plentiful and the land nearing its carrying capacity, it is inevitable that an individual animal's feeding territory frequently overlaps with those of other males. In these circumstances, the usually solitary males tolerate each other's presence and will only react with true bellicosity towards an outsider coming new to the area. These loose affiliations of male rhinos are referred to as clans and each clan lives in an area up to fifteen kms radius from the water source.

Within each clan grouping there is a dominant male and a distinct hierarchical order among the others, this order maintained by occasional ceremonial or ritual confrontations in which no animal harms another and in which antagonisms soon subside. The overthrow of a dominant bull does not cause social upheaval in the group: the vanquished leader merely leaves the clan area to try his luck with a neighbouring group.

Although often preferring solitary existences, some black rhinos will congregate together and, in these groupings, which are often associated with clans, they are quite sociable. Communication between individuals, as well as involving ritual head-flagging and facings-off against each other, can also be made through sounds.

Black rhinos have a distinct language of sounds, each with well-defined meanings. Snorting can have several interpretations: a short, sneezing 'brmph' is an alarm signal, whilst a long and deep 'hrmph' noise denotes anger, and a high-pitched squeaking sound is made when the animal is startled. When charging, an almost dog-like barking cough is frequently made. Terror is shown by a loud screaming, sometimes accompanied by a long and repetitive wailing. A mouse-like 'eak' is a calling sound used by adults to draw each other's attentions and by mothers and calves as attention and direction-finding sounds.

Black rhinos also communicate through a sort of morse code carried out by breathing sequences. These may be used to imply a welcome to another rhino, assuring it that it is accepted, or be given by one rhino to alert another of its approach. These signals are also used in conjunction with different visual cues such as ear movements, stance and position of the head.

Such communication between black rhinos is important. They need to be able to 'talk' to each other in thick bush where visibility might be reduced. Furthermore, as they are often solitary, there is a need for them to reassure each other when meeting at communal sites such as water holes.

As is to be expected, home ranges are owner-marked by middens and urine-sprayed bushes or ground.

According to the availability of food and competition for it from other rhinos, female black rhinos also maintain a feeding territory: as with the male, this might be a small area of a few square kilometres but, in semi-desert regions, territories of up to a hundred square kms have been recorded for a female accompanied by her young.

58

Quite often, the female lives with her most recent calf, sometimes with her penultimate offspring if this too was a female. They do not as a rule band together, save at communal wallows or water holes, and females are often belligerent towards other female black rhinos. As I have mentioned, upon the birth of a new calf a juvenile animal is usually forced out of its mother's range, but it does not necessarily wander off. Quite frequently, it joins forces with another of the same age and they live together in loose association until, in time, they drift apart to live a solitary existence.

Female black rhinos can be dangerous. They will readily attack an enemy in defence of their calf and, whereas males seldom fight, females may do so either when in oestrus or when protecting young. They will also attack males. At times of considerable drought or habitat loss, rhinos may fight amongst themselves, sometimes to the death, as happened in the East Tsavo section of Kenya's Tsavo game reserve in the early 1960s. This behaviour suggests that the main stress placed upon rhino numbers and society is competition for food sources: if food is plentiful then the social structure is maintained.

The black rhino's main foes are hyena, lion and elephant, the former two being the only predators to prey upon black rhino and then not upon adults but upon very young calves and occasionally younger juveniles.

Hyenas in particular, especially the spotted hyena, will hunt calves and bring them down by biting their hindquarters: the hyena is the biggest predatory threat to rhino, and successful wild breeding programmes demand the localised eradication of this animal. Lions have been known to kill calves if they can part them from their mothers, or even bring down an adult black rhino, but this is not at all a common occurrence. Lions will, however, scavenge upon rhino carcasses much as they will upon any other corpse.

Elephants kill young rhino if they consider these to be a threat to their own young, or adults if some form of confrontation occurs. Generally speaking, however, rhinos and elephants accept or at least tolerate each other.

Serious confrontations between male black rhinos are infrequent. Most common is the ritual fight which consists of the various posturings mentioned in Chapter 4. When the black rhino charges, it does so with its short tail erect, like an aerial: the white rhino leaves the tail down or allows it to hang out behind. It is also said that the black rhino will charge out of fright whilst the white does not, but I regard this as a misconception: both will attack 'from fright', which I prefer to term defensive charging.

When black rhinos most frequently fight is at the time of courtship. The female comes into oestrus approximately every four weeks at which time she is nervous and edgy and will readily attack any bull showing an interest in her. After a while, this ferocity decreases and a courtship display takes place. As the cow watches, the bull makes mock charges at bushes (which he may 'attack' and thrash frenziedly), rubs his nose and front horn on the ground, runs backwards and forwards on stiffly held legs, snorts and opens his mouth in what naturalists refer to as a 'sexual yawn', and copiously sprays urine. This display also arouses the cow, which may react violently towards it by attacking, or perform her own display, strutting on stiff legs, throwing twigs or leafy branches over her shoulder with her mouth and also mock-charging bushes. The bull, when satisfied that he will not be rejected, will then approach, his foreplay consisting of resting his head on the female's back or rump. Copulation lasts for about half an hour during which time the bull ejaculates up to a dozen or so times. Sometimes, to assist her mate, the cow will back up to a termite mound or hillock so that the bull may stand upon it, placing him in an elevated position over her rump thus allowing him easier penetration.

C.A.W Guggisberg has documented[11] fights between black rhinos of the opposite sex.

[The bull] began circling the cow, snorting continuously and twisting his tail over his rump. During most of this display the female stood as motionless as a statue. When she once turned towards [the bull] in an aggressive manner, he trampled with all four feet on the spot he stood on, looking for all the world as if he were dancing. A few moments later he launched another attack. But the cow drove him back, opening her mouth wide and uttering [a] snarling sound . . . [The bull] again rubbed his nose in the grass and shredded the surrounding bushes with his horn.

As the fight developed, the rhinos charged each other, the bull lifting the female's hindquarters clear of the ground. Eventually the cow appeared to give in.

She stood motionless, while [the bull] walked around, rubbing his nose on the ground, ploughing up the grass and tossing whole loads of branches into the air. He sprayed a bush, scraped several times (in the earth), and worked himself into such a state that he finally advanced once more upon the cow. This time she did not snarl her defiance, but retreated before him, walking backwards. [He] quietened down almost at once, and when we left the battle-field, with dusk descending on the plains, he was ambling about rather aimlessly.

Rhino society is polygamous. One female may be courted and mounted by a number of males none of whom show any sign of concern at their peers' behaviour. Mounting in the wild is not commonly observed but, in captivity, this occurs three or four times a day when the cow is in season. Whilst black rhinos are rarely seen mating in the wild, no record exists of a wild black rhino giving birth. Females conceive on average about once every three years, and up to a quarter of the females in a healthy and viable population are in breeding condition or pregnant at any one time.

As the day of birth draws near, the cow becomes reclusive and may, as mentioned, drive away her previous young: during this time she is also very restive, temperamental and dangerous. Despite the prospective mother's tetchiness, it has been observed in black rhinos that other cows will 'midwife' at a birth, supporting the expectant animal, caressing her hindquarters and accompanying her. This behaviour, more common amongst elephants which live in matriarchal groups, was noted in Nairobi game park in 1958 and has been seen twice more, once in Zambia and once in Tanzania in the 1970s.

Courtship and reproduction occur throughout the year and are not related to any seasons: unlike many African herbivores – the wildebeest, for example – and, because of its feeding habits which do not demand an itinerant life or migratory patterns, the rhino does not need to reproduce to coincide with an upsurge in food material. The bull may remain with the cow for some weeks after mating but, generally, he leaves her within a few days: bulls have been known to charge new-born calves.

The calf is born after a gestation period of about fifteen months. It weighs between thirty and forty kgs, is without horns at birth and is able to stand within minutes. The mother is very protective of her

61

young which stays close to her at all times. When threatened by a predator, the female interposes her body between the enemy and the calf, standing side on. The baby is suckled whilst the mother is standing up, supplying a very rich milk from two teats situated between her hind legs.

Although infant mortality in black rhinos (other than by predation) is rare, the young may die when teething, for reasons that remain unknown. The youngster sickens quite suddenly, its face swelling and its nose and eyes run with mucus. This illness lasts for up to a week and then clears.

The calf gains weight rapidly and by the time it has developed noticeable horns at fifteen months, it is more or less safe from predation by natural foes. Only now does it become liable to face its primary enemy, man.

Black rhino numbers are now severely depleted, and there are those naturalists who would suggest that the numbers are now too low to maintain a viable genetic bank. This argument is further strengthened by the fact that populations are now so diverse and unconnected. Only human intervention by translocation programmes can keep a gene bank going. Others are more optimistic, maintaining that, with careful protection, rhino numbers could be raised naturally. Assuming that a quarter of any population is breeding at any one time, and that the females give birth approximately every three years, this means that the population could double itself every twelve to fourteen years or so. The drawback is, of course, that the numbers might double but the rhinos would have nowhere to live save in farmland where their presence would not be welcomed.

THE WHITE RHINO

THE so-called white rhino[1] is also known as the square-lipped, or square-mouthed, or square-nosed rhino or, to a lesser extent, the grass rhino, on account of it being a grazer.

Apart from its size, the white being a good deal the bigger of the two, the main obvious difference between the white and black rhino is the upper lip. The white rhino's is wide and square without the pointed prehensile projection of the black. Furthermore, the white rhino has a pronounced ridge on its lower lip which allows it to crop grass very closely indeed: a white rhino can graze more closely than a horse. There are other differences, as shall become apparent and as have been touched upon in Chapter 4, but the shape of the mouth is certainly the most noticeable.

The animal was first scientifically recorded in South Africa by William Burchell when he discovered and made anatomical drawings of a dead specimen at Kuruman in Cape Province in 1812: it was at first known as Burchell's rhino and became widely known from 1817 when there were still reasonably large numbers extant and when Burchell came upon his first living example. However, the rapid opening up of southern Africa by white settlers soon put paid to the vast majority of the population, which was heavily hunted as a source of meat, in crop protection drives and for sport. Its habitat was quickly destroyed by farming. By 1839 it was extinct around Kuruman because it was so easy to shoot and it had begun to have an economic value which will be discussed in a later chapter.

Captain William Cornwallis Harris, another noted South and Central African explorer, saw eighty of the creatures in 1836 during a single day's trek through the Magaliesburg district of the Transvaal: Sir Andrew Smith observed over 150 rhinos in one day in the same region at about the same time. Ten years later, the French explorer, naturalist and hunter Delegorgue discovered the white rhino south of the White Umfolozi river in what was then called Zululand.

Yet, within sixty years, it had totally disappeared from Cape Province and was vanishing fast from other developing areas, especially along the coast of the Indian Ocean. In the late 1880s, Selous lamented how many animals had been killed in just that decade which he declared to be not only bad for the species but also for the environment. He probably also deplored the fact because the decline in numbers would also inhibit his sport. In 1892, he was sent after white rhino for a museum but fell from a horse whilst chasing ostrich and was injured so badly he could not continue the hunt. He later reported

> . . . the two white rhinoceros which I shot in 1882 are the last of their species that I have ever seen alive, or am ever likely to see and when I left Africa towards the end of 1892 I fully expected that these animals would become extinct within a short time . . .

and in his memoirs,[2] he wrote

> Thus it will be seen that the great square-mouthed rhinoceros, the largest of the terrestrial mammals after the elephant, which sixty years ago, was excessively common over an enormous area of country in Southern Africa to the south of 17° South latitude, and which even so lately as thirty years ago, was still very plentiful throughout many districts of that vast country, is now on the verge of extinction. . . . But that twenty of these strange, old-world creatures are alive today, I very much doubt, and in spite of game laws, which may be more or less efficient . . . I cannot think that the species will survive very far into the coming century.

Fortunately, he was wrong. Later in 1892, two of Cecil Rhodes' pioneers, Coryndon and Eyre, came upon three white rhinos although where is not exactly known: they injured the male and female and killed a calf. Three years later, Eyre killed the last white rhino bull in what was then Southern Rhodesia.

Though in evolutionary terms it is the most advanced of the two

An early sketch of a rhino – an
evil-looking beast and
a risk to virgins.

A rhino hunt by Charles Bell: the rhino is depicted
characteristically throwing its antagonist.

Rhino attacking a horse by Samuel Baker.

Capturing a black rhino using a lorry as a chase vehicle: note the lassoes on the hind legs.

A wild rhino is often identified by observers by reference to 'natural' nicks in the ears, usually caused by thorns.

The skull of a black rhino: note the dense bone structure upon which the horn is positioned, the very large nasal cavity and the comparatively small (and very well protected) brain.

A young black rhino, born in captivity in London Zoo.

Captive young black rhino head jostling: natural behaviour is
seldom curbed by captivity but may be restricted by alien
surroundings.

Black rhino, showing the prehensile upper lip used to snag branches when browsing . . .

. . . and the mouth of a white rhino showing the wide upper lip designed for grazing.

The skulls of all the black rhino poached in one year (1983–84) in the Luangwa Valley National Park, Zambia: forty have 'escaped' to die with their horns on but the remainder, over eighty (in the foreground), have had their horns axed off. Such a sight will not recur for centuries – there are now virtually no black rhino left in that park.

The final abomination: the corpse of a white rhino, killed and mutilated by poachers.

African rhinos, it has always existed in by far the lowest numbers and, until thirty years ago, it was regarded as considerably more at risk from extinction in the wild than the black rhino which, in turn, was considered not to be under significant threat. Current populations probably total in all not more than 4200 animals, although some estimates put the world population as high as 4500, perhaps even a little higher.

This total includes two apparent races of white rhino: although they are in essence the same animal, two separate populations have established themselves in historical times – the northern and the southern races. The reasons for the division of these two rhino nations, as it were, are uncertain: it may have been brought about by the human destruction of them or encroachment into suitable habitats in a broad band across equatorial Africa, or it might have been caused by native hunting. Another theory is that the division occurred in recent prehistoric time, but this cannot be proven now because there are insufficient surviving animals in the northern race to allow for genetic sampling and comparative studies to be made.

When one speaks of the white rhino one is usually referring to the southern race. The northern race, which was not discovered until 1907 when white men began to open up Uganda, formerly lived in a range across northern Zaïre, Uganda, southern Sudan and, marginally, into Chad. It is now reduced to a population of well under two dozen animals existing in the Garamba National Park in Zaïre. These are not considered to constitute a viable nucleus for natural breeding.

A few other non-viable populations existed as recently as 1980 elsewhere in Sudan and the Central African Republic, but these were exterminated by poaching in the mid-1980s and, therefore, the reader should assume that the rhino under discussion is that of the southern race.

The white rhino exists today in its largest numbers in the Republic of South Africa, not only because the majority of the area of its former natural range falls within that country but also because of the success of conservation and game management.

Despite Selous' belief of the creatures' imminent extinction in 1892, it did continue to survive albeit in very small numbers. The remnant population lived in low-lying, disease-ridden country between the Black and the White Umfolozi rivers in what are today the Umfolozi and Hluhluwe (pronounced 'Shush-looey') reserves in

Natal: in 1894, a hunting party shot six white rhinos in this area and it looked as if there would be a quick influx of avid hunters. However, the governor of Natal, Sir Walter Francis Hely-Hutchinson was a keen preserver of wildlife. He forbade the issue of shooting licences for white rhino and announced that it was to be listed as royal game – that is, protected by royal benefaction and therefore theoretically the preserve of the monarch. This, in effect, stopped them being hunted at all. In April 1897 the Umfolozi, Hluhluwe and Lake St Lucia areas were declared game reserves and closed to all hunting. This far-sighted action, begun by Hely-Hutchinson and implemented by his successor, Sir Charles Saunders, who also established a Game Conservator for Zululand, in which the reserves were positioned, saved the white rhino.

From these animals has been developed today's world population. The increase in numbers is dramatic and shows what conservation can do for an animal when a specific population is the target of regenerative protection: from an estimated thirty animals living in Umfolozi/Hluhluwe in 1930, the population there now exceeds 1750.

The second largest populations live in Zimbabwe and Botswana, for the same reasons again that these countries are in its natural range, and game control is highly efficient. Smaller populations exist in Malawi, Swaziland, Namibia, Kenya and reportedly in Zambia and Mozambique. These latter two countries may well have no populations left, due to extensive poaching activities in both countries and to the civil war that has raged in Mozambique for some years.

The probable fate of the Zambian white rhinos is well illustrated by the photograph facing page 65, a fate it must be said it shares not only with those others of its kind which live outside South Africa but also with ten of thousands of its cousin, the black rhino.

This photograph was taken in August 1988 by a close friend of mine, Keith Markham, a retired British veterinary surgeon and avid photographer. He was paying a brief visit to Victoria Falls, on the Zambian side of the Zambia/Zimbabwe border, staying at the Mosi-O-Tunya hotel right on the brink of the Falls themselves. Seeing a morning game drive advertised in the hotel, he booked himself on to it and was driven into the small Livingstone game park with several other tourists. They came upon a white rhino which had been poached during the night. The guide-cum-driver, not knowledgeable in natural history, at first thought the rhino was asleep (which it would not be doing lying on its side in the light of the rising sun), but as the vehicle drew closer to the animal the carnage was clearly seen.

The rhino had been shot within hours, the blood not yet fully congealed and no sign of decomposition had set in: the carcass did not even smell, so fresh was the killing. Its two horns had been sawn off at the very root. The remainder of the animal was abandoned. Keith Markham commenced photographing the slaughter and the driver, conscious of the bad publicity such photographs would produce, attempted to block his camera and started to drive away. With some anger, Keith Markham forced him to wait whilst he took a number of gruesome photographs.

In prehistoric times the white rhino, undivided into races, was common throughout sub-Saharan Africa and as far north as Algeria, Morocco and Tunisia. Cave paintings of the white rhino have been discovered in Tanzania, the Kalahari and the Sahara desert, but due to habitat change it has long since disappeared from these places. Desertification, which continues to increase at an alarming rate in Africa, is the most probable cause for the reduction in population numbers in ancient times.

The white rhino is the largest of all the surviving types. When fully grown, a male may be as long as 3.5 metres from nose to tail and stand nearly 1.8 metres high from the ground to the hump at the shoulders; the adult male may weigh as much as 3500 kgs, on occasion even more. Average measurements for a typical white rhino are as follows:

shoulder height	1.75 m
circumference of hind foot	86 cms
primary horn	69 cms
secondary horn	23 cms
nose to base of tail (taken over the curves as measured by hunters)	3.3 m
tail length	65 cms
ear length	25 cm
width of mouth	27 cms
body girth at widest point	3.65 m

The weight of a few of the constituent parts of an animal of this size are astounding and indicate its considerable bulk:

head	186 kgs
intestines	350 kgs
stomach	49 kgs
penis	28 kgs (and 75 cms long)

The southern race has the longest horns with some primary horns recorded at nearly two metres. Interestingly, when one considers that the horn is often used by males as symbols of strength and superiority, the females appear to grow the longer horns, but these are frequently thinner.

As with the black rhino, the primary horns have a polished appearance but whereas, in the black, this is caused by horn usage during browsing, in the white it is caused by digging. White rhinos can break their horns off doing this, the break usually occurring at or very close to the base. The attachment of the white rhino's horn seems not so firm as that of the black and begs the question that, if they were able to inhabit the earth for some considerable future, might they evolve into being hornless?

When a horn is lost, it regenerates at the rate of approximately 0.5–1 cm per month: this is, in fact, about the average rate of growth of human hair, and the comparison is not so ridiculous when one considers that the horn is, in effect, a shaped mat of hair fibres. The new horn usually reaches the length of the last.

Only those people who are fortunate enough to live or work in the few pockets of bush in which they still survive – game-rangers, wildlife photographers, conservationists and the like – are likely to have seen a wild white rhino: there are far more black rhinos in captivity than white simply because of their former abundance in the wild. This is a little surprising, however, for white rhinos are easier to keep in captivity: being grazers, they are more easily fed, can be kept in open enclosures or paddocks and they are usually comparatively docile once so confined. The white rhinos are the favourites of the drive-through safari parks of Europe because they pose little or no threat to visitors' vehicles, and they have increased in numbers in captivity over the last thirty years to such an extent that there has been an exchange or sale network of the creatures between zoos and parks. It is therefore perhaps surprising to know that it was not until 1955 that the first white rhinos came into captivity, again in London Zoo.

The white rhino is, as has been mentioned, a grazer. It predominantly eats grass, its mouth adapted to this task. The square upper lip pulls in the grass stems in much the same way as a horse's upper lip does, sweeping the material in towards the teeth. As a grazer, the white rhino is best suited to the veldt, the African grasslands in which it prefers to live. Despite liking open country, it does live part of its time in cover. This is partly a remnant of prehistoric behaviour to obtain protection from predators, but today it is primarily protection from the hot sun that it seeks. Quite often, the white rhino is found in open grassland dotted with trees or small thickets of bush, under which it takes the shade, and this seems the ideal habitat.

The white rhino, being a grazer, requires large quantities of food material, its main diet consisting of grass.[3] It cannot, as does the black rhino, vary its diet to such an extent. Furthermore, as with all rhinos, it must live near a water source for drinking, wallowing and mud-bathing. These restrictions are no doubt a substantial cause for the white rhino's natural decline. It is ill-suited to adapt to changing environments; it requires a substantial feeding territory, and it is unable to compete readily with other herbivores.

In many respects of its behaviour and life, the white rhino is similar to the black. It must drink (on average about 200 litres a day) and wallow at least every three days: it will travel some distance to water using established approach tracks: it establishes a feeding territory. However, there are also distinct differences.

The black rhino, when entering water, will walk in forwards: the white rhino, especially if the water seems deep, may go in backwards. This is not a quirk of behaviour but a valid safety mechanism: the white rhino is afraid of any expanse of wide or deep water. The black rhino can swim but white rhino cannot, and drowning is a not infrequent cause of death in some areas. By entering backwards it can prepare itself for escape.

The wallowing of the white rhino is usually conducted not in a river (as is sometimes the case with the black rhino which will bathe on the banks) but in a water hole or a pan, a shallow depression in the bush filled with water. Not surprisingly, the higher the temperature the more the rhino seeks to wallow.

On arriving at a water hole, it will test the depth before moving in until the water reaches the belly. The rhino then drinks its fill before the water becomes too muddied by movement or wallowing activity. It may lie in the water for several hours, moving slightly every twenty minutes or so.

The next stage, the mud-wallowing, involves the rhino sticking its nose and horn well into the mud, submerging its face to the eyes. It will then lie in the mud and roll from side to side, sometimes almost rolling completely on to its back: the mud can support this action which, on dry land, the rhino finds extremely difficult if not impossible. This done, the rhino lies in the mud for up to two hours, depending upon the heat of the day, sometimes shifting to a new patch of mud and commencing all over again. When the rhino has finished wallowing, it moves into nearby shade to let the mud cool and harden slowly. In common with the black rhino, the white also sand- and dust-bathes.

Unlike the white rhino, the black holds its head up moving about its territory: the white keeps its head lowered as if it were feeding, only raising it when danger beckons. They can reach a speed of about forty kms per hour, not quite as fast as the black rhino, and they cannot keep up this speed for as long as their smaller relative: they also take a longer distance to reach top speed. They are, however, very agile considering their bulk, and can climb over obstacles of two metres height or more: the black would prefer to ram its way through an obstacle and would not so readily consider an attempt at climbing.

During the hot season of the year, the white rhino feeds predominantly at night, dozing and lying up in the shade during the middle of the day: this nocturnal feeding is not established because of human hunting, as has been suggested in the case of the black rhino. When the cooler weather breaks, and during the rains, the white rhino feeds and dozes alternately through the twenty-four-hour cycle. When extensively parasitised and bothered by flies, the white rhino often stands in open places where a breeze will blow the insects away. As well as mud-bathing and dust-rolling to kill parasites they also have trees and rocks which are established communal scratching-poles: around a wallowing centre many of the trees, usually of a hardwood variety, are barked and worn smooth by years of usage. These scratching-places, when away from communal wallows, also act as boundary scent-markers for an individual's territory.

As in the case of the black rhino, the white is territorial, the area of an individual's range being generally greater than that of a black rhino. This is hardly surprising when it has such a comparatively small variety of plants upon which to feed.

A white rhino's territory is seldom less than two square kilometres, even where food is very plentiful, and it may often be much greater depending upon population density, the availability of food and the presence of water. Territories are marked by middens but whereas the black rhino male kicks his dung about at these sites, in white rhinos only the territorial owning male does so. Other visitors merely deposit their droppings on or near the midden or in piles beside known and established rhino paths to water. In addition, urine is frequently sprayed – sometimes as often as every few minutes, especially where populations are at their most dense – at territorial boundaries and, as mentioned, rubbing-posts give added information as to territorial proprietorship.

The structure of white rhino society is somewhat similar to that of the black in that the males and females have separate patterns of social interaction.

Males retain feeding territories which they seek to maintain for themselves, the range becoming also a breeding territory when courtship and mating occurs. At this time, both male and female will defend it. Within an area, one male becomes paramount. He will drive away other mature males but he will allow juveniles to feed in his range, challenging them only when they near full maturity. A fully mature but subordinate male may also be allowed to share the territory on condition that he does not challenge his superior's position and he proves his subordination from time to time by submission after a confrontation, by not urine-spraying and by ceasing to deposit his dung on the landowner's middens. He also signals his inferiority by whine-grumbling after each conflict, a noise beyond description in words. These confrontations, when they occur, seldom involve an actual fight and the occasion of white rhino bulls doing actual physical harm to each other is very rare indeed, even in conflicts over mating. More commonly observed are trials of prowess and strength involving horn wrestling, mock-charging, shoulder-barging and occasionally bush-thrashing.

The white rhino charges with its tail down or held out horizontally, but when running from another rhino, or escaping in fear from or reacting to a perceived threat, the tail is raised and arched over like a comic-strip pig's: this is also the position it is placed in when dunging.

In due course, the tolerated males will tumble the dominant animals from their thrones and take over their territories.

Females are also territorial but maintain considerably larger personal areas than the males. These invariably overlap with male domains but no confrontations occur at all. Furthermore, females' territories frequently protrude into each other and yet still no conflict happens.

Once again, as with the males and black rhinos, water holes and mud wallows are communal property. Upon giving birth, females reject their penultimate offspring which establish bonds with other peers or with childless females which, where the land is at or near its carrying capacity, may gather a number of 'step-children'. Unlike the black rhino which tends to be solitary, the white rhino may live in small groups of up to ten individuals, usually a loose confederation of juveniles and females.

Confrontations between black and white rhinos are infrequent, even where there are many animals living in a small area as, say, in a finite reserve. This is not surprising as the two types do not interbreed and are not in competition for food or habitat.

Breeding amongst white rhinos differs from that of the black rhino. Although mating occurs without regard to the seasons, as in the case of the black rhino, there is a marked incidence of increased activity after the rains when the food supply is abundant and fresh. The cow matures at the age of seven or eight and comes into oestrus approximately six months after the birth of her previous calf, whilst she is still in milk: she will come into oestrus on average every six weeks when she is not pregnant, the periodicity varying from animal to animal. She announces her condition by walking through the territory of dominant males, urine-spraying and therefore chemically marking her presence and receptibility.

Courtship rituals last longer than those of the black rhino – as much as three weeks – because the female may attack the male during his approaches and, if she still has one in attendance, so might her calf, which may well be of a substantial size but still very possessive of its mother: calves are not completely weaned until at least a year old. On the other hand, a courting bull will try to insinuate himself between the cow and her offspring and, if successful,

72

will himself drive the calf off. This behaviour, however, tends to occur only where the calf is a juvenile rather than a recently weaned youngster.

Males retain females within their territories by chasing them towards centre grounds, often whining loudly. Any intruding dominant males intent on mating will be driven off. The males may also kill calves and this leads to the females being increasingly protective of their young which they guard closely from birth, as does the black rhino. A female in season amongst a group of other cows and juveniles can cause her companion females to form a defensive circle, calves in the centre and mothers around, facing outwards with heads lowered in threat. At the time, the females paw at the ground and snort defiantly.

As the courtship process progresses, the female becomes less belligerent until eventually copulation occurs. This may be prolonged for up to thirty minutes and be repeated every hour or so for as long as twenty-four hours, although copulation infrequently happens at night. Mating over, the female will leave the male's territory with her calf: if, however, she has no attendant youngster, she may remain in the male's home range, establishing a loose pair-bonding with him and, sometimes, defending his territory in collaboration with him. Females mate approximately every third year and can live to the age of about fifty, bearing young into old age.

Such a breeding rate is slow and may well account for the low numbers of white rhinos, despite the lack of predation and the fact that infant mortality figures are insignificant.

The white rhino's gestation period is sixteen months and the birth is of a single infant: twin births have been recorded but they are extremely rare. The cow drops her newborn in solitude, usually in cover.

Like the black rhino, the white is not a silent animal but has a fairly large repertoire of noises which are not merely expressive but also believed to be communicative.

When unexpectedly meeting, adults pant-cough at each other from some way off, while juveniles whine and squeal to their mothers. Dominant males threaten adversaries with low-pitched grumblings, which may escalate into a full-bellied bellowing, which in turn may become a loud and eerie screaming. After confrontations, the loser utters a sort-of chirrup as he retreats. Courting males, as has been noted, wail but also make what is best described as a throbbing hiccupping, which some observers suggest is akin to the low frequency growls with which elephants communicate over long distances. Its function during courtship is unknown. Quite often, when surrogate mothers with 'adopted' juveniles or rejectees meet at a communal venue – a water hole, say – the youngsters often greet each other with little pig-like squeals and gruntings which lead to what might be interpreted as play-wrestling.

Whenever one sees a white rhino in the wild, one cannot escape the impression of size, of incredible benign strength and of a strange inner passiveness. The creature looks peaceful, amiable and secure. If a creature can be said to have discovered transcendental meditation, then it must be the white rhino. They have about themselves a distinct aura of calm and I have to admit to finding them quite pacifically beautiful. Yet I have seen them in another light: not charging malevolently – I have never been seriously charged by either a wild black or white rhino – or stomping and pawing the ground with bull-like suppressed anger, but rather cavorting like lambs in a field, chasing each other like puppies. I have to add, however, that the ground shook.

The future of the white rhino is doubtful. The northern race, in particular, seems doomed. However, there is a slender chance that there may be small numbers living in the wild that are unaccounted for: the Murchison Falls National Park in Uganda, for example, may house some specimens and there may well be others living in isolated pockets in Sudan and northern Zaïre, unknown because civil wars or a collapse of local government have made it impossible for surveys to be taken.

I secretly harbour the hope that there are some unknown, small yet viable white rhino groups existing, paradoxically protected by war. After all, a number of Javan rhinos, thought to have been extinct save for a very small population in the Udjung Kulon National Park in western Java, were discovered in November 1988 in the Dong Nai river valley of Vietnam, saved not by conservationists but by the Vietnam War which rendered their territory inaccessible.

— 7 —

IN RHINO COUNTRY

FOR all that one might write about the rhino, its natural history and the intricate details of its life, there is nothing like meeting the animal on its home range to drive in the real notion of what the creature is like; and, if one cannot actually fly to Africa for a head-to-head rendezvous, the next best thing is to hear of others' encounters.

It is impossible, in mere words, to capture adequately the thrill of seeing for the first time an especially sought-after animal in the wild, particularly if it is one of the African Big Five, as the hunters first dubbed them – lion, leopard, elephant, rhino or buffalo. It is a highlight of one's life to come across any of these and the sight of a pride of lions from the interior of a saloon car or safari vehicle is no less reduced by the knowledge of one's comparative safety behind steel panels and in command of a speedy escape.

Yet nothing can beat the excitement and sheer, unadulterated exhilaration of first meeting one of these wondrous animals on its own terms, in its own territory and under its own set of rules and codes of behaviour. To do that, one has to be on foot.

To walk for the first time in the African bush is an experience no one ever forgets: even those for whom such an experience becomes commonplace, an hour thus spent in the bush never lacks its charm, vitality and thrill. Any fear of whatever danger exists is soon over-come – but advisedly never forgotten or ignored – by the sheer wonder of the charm of the unsullied natural world. To track a rhino is perhaps the subject of the ultimate walk in the bush.

I have, on a number of occasions, had the inestimable good fortune to go after rhino in the wild. I have never hunted one with the intention of killing it, and have no desire so to do: for me, the thrill of any hunt is not stalking an animal to kill but placing myself

75

on equal terms to the quarry, pitting my feeble wits against its own in the hope of a trophy – a close-up photograph taken without a long focus lens.

Indeed, I have never gone after rhino with any weapon. I have been accompanied by others who have been armed, but with guns that are not intended to kill or are even capable of more than lightly wounding: their object is to frighten. Having said that, I have never seen one of these discharged.

Needless to say, despite my long experience of being in the bush, my encounters with rhinos have been few and far between, partly due to my own bungling, partly due to their artful skills of survival, and partly due to the sad fact that there are not so many of them now left around in the wild.

The tracking of any wild animal is difficult, be it an English fox or an African lion, demanding considerable tolerance and patience as well as knowledge and tested expertise. Wild creatures know what men are capable of and they give human beings a wide berth whenever they can. What is more, they are in their element, alert to all possibilities and able to decide the course of action of any encounter. In other words, the balance is tipped markedly in their favour.

A wild animal relies upon its advanced senses, its instincts, which I believe can at times amount almost to a telepathic capability, and its experience to survive. A man has lost the acute edge to his senses and his instincts are atrophied. Only when the man has a gun is he superior to the quarry he is stalking.

It follows that, with the odds loaded very much in the animal's favour, it is the animal which calls most if not all of the moves of the game. This being the case means that the man is not only inferior but vulnerable and potentially in a dangerous situation.

More often than not, however, the animal will decide against a meeting and there is nothing the man can do about it. He will simply be left alone on the stage. If the animal decides that it wants, or has been forced into a confrontation, then it will attack and, without his gun, the man has only two options – to stand and take the chance that the attack is for show rather than for real, and perhaps be injured or killed, or to take flight.

Tracking black rhino can be particularly difficult and hazardous: because the animal lives in thick cover, it is very difficult to approach silently. The crickle of dried leaves and twigs underfoot, the pushing aside of snagging thorned branches and the alarms of unseen birds all inform the rhino of the tracker's proximity. The rhino itself is exceptionally difficult to see. Its grey hide, often blotched with dried mud flakes, is superbly camouflaged. In the dense cover, the wind direction may shift unaccountably and unnoticeably, thus giving the rhino more information.

In 1989, I stalked black and white rhino in northern Natal in the company of Ron Thomson, his son and his brother Ian, a senior game warden with the KwaZulu game department. We were in the Ndumu reserve primarily to see white rhino but came upon the scrape-marks of a black rhino by the side of a bush road. These had been made all along the verge of the track at intervals of about twenty metres and were only minutes old.

It being mid-morning, we left the Land Rover under the shade of some trees and entered first a large clearing the size of a tennis court that was plainly a small water hole in the wet season: the ground was hard, sun-baked mud embedded with well-worn tracks of a variety of animals. The rhino, having marked its territory on the road, had crossed this dried pan and entered the surrounding thick thorn bush.

The cover was close but not really dense. We could see about ten metres ahead through the pale trunks of small thorn trees that were all about the thickness of a strong man's forearm, and three or four metres tall. Noting such detail becomes important when tracking rhino: the only safe place to be when charged is up a tree. The ground was thick with dried twigs and covered with brittle leaves over which the occasional lizard scampered.

On account of the low canopy of the thorn trees, we had to walk half bent with our heads held back to see forwards. We had to be particularly careful where we placed our feet and obeyed the rule that is often the best when tracking in numbers – step where the man in front had trod. This reduces sound somewhat: on loose sand it makes progress easier.

The rhino could have been anywhere. There was no discernible wind, although the direction of the minute breeze was divined with a handful of fine dust: it was blowing towards us, head-on.

For about ten minutes, we moved into the breeze, taking great care to be utterly silent. This was not easy. The leaf litter was exceptionally noisy and the entire cover consisted of thorn bushes which bore iron-hard spikes up to seven cms long and as sharp as hypodermic needles. Many thorny twigs had fallen to the ground and, when trodden on, not only cracked loudly but pierced even leather.

We were not following the rhino's spoor but had assessed roughly where it would be by the direction of the tracks at the water hole, the passage of time since it had entered the cover and the knowledge that, on hearing the Land Rover, the rhino would have headed for the densest scrub which lay ahead of us. We need not have listened for her progress: a rhino can choose to move silently over even the most noisy of terrains.

Suddenly, Ian stopped and hand-signalled behind his back. We froze. The rhino was not ten metres ahead, to the right front, standing three-quarters on to us, head down and ears alert. The animal was a cow with a youngster of just a few months old standing behind her, most of it out of sight.

I was given this information in a very muted whisper by Ron, his lips brushing my ear, for I could not see a square centimetre of the rhino despite her proximity and size. I could smell her and I could hear a gentle, deep and infrequent pant of breath yet I could not so much as make out one detail of her huge body.

She stamped her foot. We all instinctively looked around for a tree trunk to climb: if you can get two metres above ground, you are more or less safe. The black rhino charges with head down and does not generally look up for its enemy when in dense cover. If she decided to come at us, we would have to ignore the lacerating thorns and thrust ourselves heedlessly up through the vicious branches.

There was no other sound save her occasional breathing. No birds sang, no crickets chirruped, no other creatures moved in the undergrowth. The sunlight under the canopy of thorn branches was diluted and soft.

The breeze shifted capriciously. Her scent disappeared. Again, she stamped her foot and snorted briefly: it appeared as if she was now scenting us. Ian signalled a hasty but controlled retreat. We set off stepping backwards. I raised my camera to my face and took one photo of the area of dense cover in which the rhino was standing. It was only then that I saw her and then only the top half of her left ear as it moved to pick up the click of the camera shutter. Although it was hard to tell in the tangle of trunks and thorns she was, I reckoned, approximately 1.50 metres high at the shoulder and about eight metres away.

That such a huge animal can be so close and yet be so completely invisible is one of the marvels of the bush.

The following day, we went in search of white rhino.

White rhino, living as they do in more open country, are easier to see in the distance. Nevertheless, the eye must be attuned to recognising their shape against the backdrop of bush. Unless they are standing on an open plain or in direct sunlight and far from cover, their outline is easily broken up, much as a military vehicle might be hidden by painting it in random patterns of different neutral colours. Once again, their grey skin patched with mud, dust or leaves affords them a degree of invisibility. But approaching them is easier, and requires less stalking.

The first white rhino we came upon was a lone bull standing side on to us in a small clearing of grass tussocks. He was chewing with all the meditative calm of a Jersey cow in a field. We walked towards him, halting about fifty metres away. The wind was to our advantage and the sun coming over our right shoulders. He was not oblivious to our presence but it did not appear to concern him unduly.

I found it hard to assess his size. There was nothing by which to measure him. His bulk was nevertheless impressive, his shoulder surmounted by a powerful solid hump. His front, primary horn was thick at the base but tapered very quickly to a much thinner, longer point. He may well have been stropping it quite recently for the base was covered in red earth. The rearmost, secondary horn was little more than a round smooth bump.

With a slow and graceful ease, he turned to face us. His ears ranged in our direction. Then without any hurry, he turned and walked away into the bushes. As soon as the rhino was gone, Ron walked to the spot where he had been and stood on the rhino's front footprint. Judging from Ron's height, we guessed the bull to have been 1.86 metres high to the top of his hump, his primary horn 41 cms long from the root.

An hour later we came upon a rare sight, four white rhinos grazing together on a grassy plain dotted about by individual thorn trees and aloe plants. The group appeared from some sparse woodland and, over the space of a quarter of an hour, moved into full view. The group consisted of a male, two females and a juvenile.

Such a grouping together might well have been accounted for in Ndumu because of the density of the population. A closed 100

79

square kilometre block of bush, and encompassed within a steel-link elephant-proof fence and electrified trip wire, it is a reserve set aside especially for the breeding of wild rhinos: the land is near its carrying capacity and the success of the rhino breeding programme is due to the localised eradication of hyena, the main killer of infant rhinos, and the considerable thinning out of other major predators. When I was there, the population stood at forty-eight black and fifty-three white rhinos in the reserve.

Once again, these creatures paid scant heed to our presence of which they were aware. The breeze was shifting direction at will and from time to time, the rhinos must have scented us. We did not need to crouch to get near to them but walked slowly forwards upright, only keeping an occasional tree trunk or aloe between the nearest animal and ourselves.

The rhinos were grazing upon the fresh growth of grass that had come through where a controlled burning had been allowed to bring down the long dry season stems. Every so often one or other of the rhinos would cease feeding and turn its head towards us, swivelling its ears, but otherwise they ignored us.

Gradually, we drew closer, moving in a line abreast and going down into a semi-squat to reduce our outlines.

At about twenty metres from the nearest rhino, we stopped. This is close to the white rhino's threshold in open country: to go nearer is to risk a confrontation. By way of confirming this, the male sprayed a short burst of urine against an aloe. The jet was as fine as that from an aerosol. It did not drip from the dead aloe leaves.

Crouching low, I expended some ten rolls of film on the animals before allowing them gradually to move away into the distance.

The male of this group was a good deal bigger than the lone animal. He was nearer 1.95 metres at the shoulder and his primary horn was very long and pointed, a scimitar which curved back in a smooth, thin blade at least 60 cms from root to tip. It, too, appeared to have been regularly stropped: perhaps the population density in the area meant that males frequently confronted each other over territory and that horn-stropping and ground-rubbing was a frequent convention in their lives. His secondary horn, though a third of the size of the other, was also sharp.

The females' horns were shorter and fatter but still sharp, whereas the juvenile, aged between two and three years, had a pronounced primary horn with a secondary one just a bump.

Leaving these fabulous creatures to drift away from us was for me a sorrow. I wanted to remain in their company, follow them through the day, watch them go about their peaceable way of life, continue to marvel at them.

Not all rhino encounters, of course, are as genial. The rhino has earned its reputation of being irascible, contrary, sometimes unpredictable and on occasion downright terrifying.

In an attempt to combat rhino poaching and to establish populations in areas away from the threat of both poaching and habitat loss, it was decided in the late 1960s by what was then the Rhodesian government (now Zimbabwe) to carry out a programme of translocation.

'Operation Rhino' involved the live capture of black rhinos by darting them with tranquillisers in the northern part of the country and Hwange (known at that time as Wankie) National Park, then transporting them by lorry to the Gonarhezhou reserve in the south, on the border with Mozambique. This astonishing programme, one of the first of its kind but which has since been frequently repeated in various parts of Africa, was organised by Ron Thomson and Paul Coetsee. The following encounter was recorded by John Gordon Davis in his book on the translocation programme[1] and occurred in the region of Umfurudzi, north-east of Harare.

. . . Ahead, thirty paces, two trees stood well apart above the tall grass. The rhino probably lay under one of them.

Coetsee crept down the trail. It took a turn in the high grass and then ahead lay an area of sparse grass, forty paces wide, and then the thick grass started again. Just in the thick grass across the open space stood the tree, and under the tree, in a small dust-bowl, stood the rhino. He stood with his massive hindquarters into the small hot wind so he could scent what was approaching him from behind and see what was coming from the front, and hear what was coming from all sides. He was dozing, head down in the shade, sideways on to Coetsee, and Coetsee could just see the top ridge of his great back and the tip of his horn through the grass.

Coetsee signalled to Kapesa and Richard to come up, fast and quiet. Then he signalled to Kapesa to go twenty paces through the grass, to the edge of the sparse area. He signalled Richard to stay where he was with the .458. Coetsee pulled out his ash-bag

81

and tested the wind. It still lay as the beast was indicating. Coetsee stared at the beast. Then he left the cover of the elephant grass and he entered the sparse area.

He ran crouched down on tiptoe, expertly silent through the sparse yellow grass in the open, straight at the beast that would kill him with one throw, ran to take the beast by surprise, to have the advantage of initiative, to put it in the position where it had to deploy to his tactics and not vice versa; to force his decision on it. Coetsee ran straight at the beast, crosswind, through the tall sparse grass, ten, fifteen, twenty paces, twenty-five, and the beast heard him and it turned.

It spun around with a huff and a snort, vicious, startled, on guard, as tall as Coetsee and a dozen times as heavy, with deadly armour, whirling round, red-eyed, snorting to kill and Coetsee stopped dead. He could not get a safe shot through the tall grass, he wanted to get a reliable flank shot and he stopped dead and stared at the animal, panting and sweating. They stared at each other, blue eyes staring out red eyes rolling wild, astonished; Coetsee stood there, crouched, panting, and stared the beast out, and the great beast gave a furious roar and dropped its head wild-eyed and charged. Charged thundering, snorting, great black head down and Coetsee just stood there, crouched, sweating, staring as the beast came charging, it came thundering straight at him, and stopped. It thundered to a halt ten paces from the man and the dust puffed up round its great feet and it snorted, puffing wild-eyed, at the man and it jerked its great head, red-eyed, and Coetsee just stood. Then it backed off to charge again.

It backed off huffing, head down, eyes wild, lumbering backwards through the elephant grass gathering its great armoured bulk to charge again. It lumbered back ten paces and Coetsee just stood there, staring the animal in the eye, concentrating all his will-power on it, and the beast snorted once more and then charged. The earth shook, it came thundering through the grass down on Coetsee to kill, and Coetsee stood, and it came thundering, snorting, red-eyed, to a halt again. It stood there, great flanks heaving, glaring, and Coetsee stood crouched, staring at it. He did not raise the gun. The movement would have broken the spell, the something between them, the man imposing his will, his presence, his superiority. That would have been broken and the beast would have charged all the way and Coetsee only had a dart-gun. The rhino stood, huffed and puffed, for five seconds, ten paces off, then it backed off again for the final charge.

Coetsee crouched there willing Kapesa and the beast and himself, waiting for Kapesa to create a diversion so he could get a flank shot. The beast lumbered back snorting through the grass, glaring at Coetsee; it stood one moment, gathering its huge self and then it charged, and Kapesa acted. The beast charged at Coetsee and thirty yards behind Kapesa stepped out of the elephant grass to show himself and clapped his hands once and the beast saw him and swerved to charge Kapesa. It swerved in full charge and thundered headlong at Kapesa and Coetsee pivoted as the two-thousand-pound beast thundered past him five paces away pounding the earth, and he slapped a dart into him. There was a crack of the cartridge in the pounding of the earth and the silver dart with the red, white and blue fletches smacked in to the great galloping rump, and Kapesa was running for the tree. He got to it ten paces ahead of the animal, it gave a great toss of its head at the tree trunk, and then it crashed on into the elephant grass, the silver dart flashing in its side, and it disappeared.

Maybe the whole business had taken sixty seconds.

There is a more than a modicum of story-teller's licence in this passage, a very heavy ladling of the stuff of ripping yarns: rhinos can hardly be said to go 'red-eyed with rage', they are not armoured and they do not so much roar as grunt loudly and sonorously. Yet it is a fair illustration of a rhino at bay and charging. It describes the preliminary mock-charging with which the rhino hopes to deter its opponent from a real fight, the pauses to assess the situation and its adversary, the staring sessions which rhinos use between themselves when facing off each other and the earth-shaking charge. It also shows the considerable skill, knowledge and bravery of those who would risk their lives to save the rhino.

It is not unknown for rhinos to charge in a seemingly perverse fashion. However, they are not naturally aggressive and will attack only when the rules of etiquette, territory or conflict have been infringed. Most often, it is the charged victim who has unwittingly contravened the code. For this reason, rhinos have been known to attack cars and other vehicles.

In the early days of the construction of the railway through Kenya towards Uganda, rhinos attacked trains. That they were (and are) not averse to charging road vehicles has already been mentioned but this habit is not recent.

Commander Simon van der Stel, one of the earliest explorers of southern Africa, records[2] a rhino attack on his Cape expedition of 1685/6. On 4 September 1685, as the expedition approached the Piketberg range about 120 kms north of Cape Town, the procession came upon a rhinoceros of 'incredible size' which allegedly became suddenly enraged. It charged directly at van der Stel's horse-drawn carriage. The commander grabbed a blunderbuss, which would have proved inefficient in any case, and leapt from his carriage to avoid the impact. As the rhino charged, van der Stel took aim at it but the mechanism in his gun jammed. He was now at the mercy of the charge. A quick-witted soldier in the expedition fired at the rhino which he hit in the belly. This caused the rhino to swerve and it ran past van der Stel 'just grazing his side'. Another expedition member wrote that, had it not been for the soldier's presence of mind, the rhino would have 'crushed and devoured the Honourable Commander'. (Had this been the case, it would have been the only record of a carnivorous rhino: such a statement indicates the ignorance existing of these animals, such misconceptions continuing today.) Injured, the rhino blundered about, charging and injuring horsemen and their mounts. What subsequently became of the rhino is not reported.

For most people these days, African game is only viewed from a vehicle. Walking safaris are few and far between and often the preserve of the richer-than-average tourist requiring considerable individual organisation, man-power and labour-intensive tented camps: what is more, the Big Five are not likely to be caught up with on foot by those unused to the ways of the bush. A vehicle, though perhaps somewhat 'tame' is not necessarily a disadvantage: it affords not only a means of rapid retreat from danger but also a comfortable, comparatively safe and mobile hide, sometimes affording a very close approach to otherwise cautious animals.

Wild animals do not usually associate vehicles with mankind. I have been within five metres of a pride of lions whilst sitting in an open Land Rover without so much as a windscreen between myself and the lions. So long as one does not move suddenly, does not stand up and does not speak, the animals remain ignorant of the presence of men. The smell of the vehicle stifles or confuses the human scent and the vehicle becomes a mobile ant-hill or (in the case of the lions) a foul-smelling, inedible big animal. To the rhino, however, a large vehicle, unscented but vaguely seen, might well be interpreted as another big herbivore providing competition for food. As such, it will not be tolerated.

Viewing rhino from a vehicle can be almost as exciting as meeting one on foot. Whilst on a photographic and anthropological expedition in the 1950s, the American explorer, William Morden, and his wife, Irene, met a black rhino and experienced[3] how these creatures may react towards a safari car.

On that first day, as we were driving slowly here and there, pausing now and again to shoot a few feet of film and then moving on, to our delight we chanced upon a big rhino that was quite unaware of our presence. Mtunga was at the wheel, and Harry was beside him, while the two of us were in the second seat, ready to use the camera either from where we sat or through the [roof] hatch. We stopped immediately, with the safari car headed towards the rhino. He was in a large burnt-over patch and had apparently been rolling in it. For he was as grey as the ashes of the burnt grass and the wind was swirling little eddies of ash dust. We were at some distance from him and the light was not right for a good shot. We also needed to be closer to keep the dust from blurring our pictures.

As the wind seemed about right to keep the rhino from catching our scent. Mtunga shifted into low and we crept ahead, making remarkably little noise, though there was a low hum of gears and the soft sound of the car's exhaust. We did not drive directly towards him, but edged off a little to one side. The idea was to shorten the distance and change the angle of the light. The old fellow didn't make a move even when we had come within fifty yards of him. That was close enough and we stopped, but kept the engine idling, with the car headed a little towards the right of where he stood. The light was good, too. It only remained for Bill to stand up, to push the camera through the hatch, focus it, and set it going.

We were still down wind. Or rather we thought we were. Perhaps the wind shifted, or possibly an eddy in the breeze played us a trick and carried our scent to him. At any rate, he suddenly shifted his head and his tail went up like a battle flag. He snorted prodigiously. Then he snorted again. Dropping his head and pointing his horn at us, he charged!

In all Africa no animal gives a greater impression of awkwardness than an unsuspicious rhino. But let him drop his head, raise his tail, and charge, and there is nothing whatever awkward about him. He is fast. He is powerful. And he means business. It is often said that his charge is merely a rhino's way of investigating something that his poor eyesight makes it impossible for him to see clearly. That may be. We don't pretend to know. No rhino has ever taken us into his confidence.

'Let's go!' shouted Harry.

But that wasn't so easy. The trouble was with the way the car was headed. We had to make a turn, and the rhino was able to cut across lots while we were making it. Mtunga, by the grace of all his African gods, didn't kill that engine. He let in the clutch and stepped hard on the accelerator. We were thrown heavily back into our seats. This was a race we are not likely to soon forget.

Mtunga could see all the bumps, for the grass was gone, but he couldn't miss all of them. And he dared not go too fast, lest he break a spring, or bounce us out, or lose control of the careening car.

This unpleasant little fiasco had begun with the rhino some fifty yards away. But that distance had been sharply cut, when Mtunga made the quickest kind of a turn. At last the car was headed away and, in the back seat, we were doing our best to keep our eyes on the charging animal. This was hard to do. We had to hang out of the car in order to look back, and the bumps didn't help a bit. We were now moving at twenty-five miles or more an hour, with an enormous cloud of ashy dust behind us – a cloud so dense that it was hard to see the rhino through it. Now and again we had a glimpse of him. There he was, plunging along through the dust no more than fifty or sixty feet behind us and showing no signs whatever of losing his enthusiasm.

The situation may have had its humorous side. At that moment we failed to see it. If we hit some really serious chuckhole it would not have been funny at all. But thanks to Mtunga and the sturdiness of the Dodge safari car – and thanks, too, to a providential absence of chuckholes – we began to pull away from our cantankerous pursuer. Then, by accident or design, Mtunga brought the chase to an end.

86

He changed his course a little, and he changed it abruptly. The rhino, all but hidden in the dust cloud, was unable to make us out. He was still coming along with undiminished speed, but he was apparently following a straight line in a half-blind way. Consequently, when he reached the point at which Mtunga had changed direction, he suddenly found himself in clear air again. He didn't stop charging. He went right on, even though we were no longer ahead of him. We were well off to one side, and though we were still a little in advance, we were running on a course parallel to his. The light was right, too, and Mtunga began to slow down. Then we were at last able to get the camera into action.

Little by little, as we photographed him, the rhino slowed up. From a fast trot he dropped into a slower one. From a trot he slowed down to a walk. Finally he stopped. It was as simple as that. He stopped, and for a moment stood looking about. Then he dropped his tail, took a few steps towards a bush, and then as if nothing had occurred to upset him, he began to browse.

The most exciting observations of a wild animal are often gained by watching it not as a participant in the action as the Mordens were but as a third party bystander.

C.A. Spinage was a police officer in Kenya who, during his time in the bush in action against the Mau Mau insurgents, became entranced by the fauna and subsequently dedicated his life to being a naturalist. He spent much of his time studying all the East African wild animals to write both authoritatively but in layman's terms about them later. On one instance, he records[4] a contretemps between a black rhino and lion:

While I was driving around on the floor of the Ngorongoro Crater in Tanganyika an example of the reluctance of the Lion to exert itself was demonstrated to me. A Rhinoceros appeared to be very interested in a pair of black-maned Lions that were quietly resting out in the open. When I arrived on the scene the Rhino also showed a lively interest in me, so I thought that I would hurry things up by driving round behind the Lions to see what would happen. In this position I waited as the Rhino gradually worked its way towards them, bending its head this way and that as it tried to get a clear view. I expected the Lions to take the offensive and was surprised to see that, when the Rhino arrived within about twenty feet, they began to snarl and grunt their displeasure. Undaunted the Rhino plodded forward, head lowered and horns presented ready for trouble. Surely its death was imminent? But no: with more snarling and grunting, the Lions suddenly got up and slunk out of the way, whereupon the Rhino made a short rush at them and they ran off!

But more was yet to come. Not far away another large, black-maned Lion was resting with its Lioness, and the Rhino now made unerringly towards them. Much the same preliminary procedure then followed as it slowly plodded forward, turning its head this way and that, twitching its ears and blowing down its nostrils, until it was within a few feet.

This time the Lioness was the first to start expressing displeasure by grunting and snarling, and then, of all things, she went through motions similar to those performed amongst Lions preliminary to mating. At these demonstrations the male became very aggressive, and began to run backwards and forwards snarling and grunting. Suddenly it rushed over to one of the other Lions that happened to be walking along quite quietly about thirty yards away. Rearing up at it the former snarled and snapped ferociously but, terrifying as this display seemed to the onlooker, the attacked Lion did not seem greatly impressed, merely snarling back and walking away. The Lion then rushed back to his Lioness, and by this time the Rhino was almost on top of them. At this point the Lioness suddenly got up and moved off, followed by the male. Again the Rhino made a rush at them to hurry them on their way, and after following for a little gave up and continued grazing. The Lion and his mate then sat down as if nothing had happened!

George Adamson, the famous lion conservator and husband of Joy Adamson, came upon another encounter between rhinos and lions when hunting man-eaters in Samburu tribal lands in the late Thirties. He wrote[5]:

By the end I had to shoot six [man-eating lions], one of which I hunted for three days. Each time Lembirdan [his native tracker] and I got close to him we found he was lying in a bush close to a rhino. If it had happened once I would have said that it was a coincidence but when it happened three times I was convinced that the lion had deliberately sought the rhino's company. It probably felt it would give him a warning if someone approached, though of course it was the oxpeckers [tick-birds] which provided the tip-off, with the loud hissing noise they make on such occasions. It is strange that these birds, when perched on domestic cattle, ignore the presence of people.

One has to express the wish that men might learn to co-exist with so little friction.

African colonial writing is rich with tales of rhino encounters. Captain C.R.S. Pitman, a game warden in Uganda in the 1930s, records[6] a number of these: a missionary was driving a car along a bad road when a white rhino calf appeared before him. Knowing it to be a mild animal, he stopped to avoid hitting it. Suddenly, however, the cow appeared and sniffed at the car. The missionary, somewhat perturbed, drove slowly forwards and the calf gave way running along in front of the vehicle. The cow fell in line behind the car, snorting and trotting after it. Only when the calf stepped into the bush did the cavalcade cease.

Not all such encounters were as innocuous. Pitman quotes a District Officer who, believing himself to be the object of a charge, threw his gun to his shoulder to 'perpetrate the unpardonable crime of deliberately shooting' a white rhino. He pulled the trigger only to hear it click: the gun was unloaded. The rhino swerved aside at a few paces from him and ran away. The result would have been fatal had the gun gone off: the rhino might have been killed and the man almost assuredly would have been, if only by being struck by the bulk of a dead rhino.

Records show that black rhinos are reported to have killed more people than white rhinos. This is not an indication that they are necessarily more ferocious. Living in dense cover, they are more likely to be stumbled upon unawares and therefore provoked. Additionally, until very recent times, black rhino have massively out-numbered the white so it follows that they would be statistically more prominent in records.

Often, it has been error that has led to an injury or fatality: for example, the famous white hunter and early conservationist, Charles Cottar, was killed by a black rhino on 7 September 1940 in the Siana Hills of the Masai Mara (in Kenya) whilst attempting to cine-film a black rhino. The rhino, breaking from dense cover, charged Cottar who, camera to eye, misjudged its distance through the viewfinder. Dropping the camera too late, he managed to shoot the rhino twice before it gored him. The rhino was killed. Cottar survived the charge, but with a torn femoral artery. He died shortly afterwards, beside the rhino, from loss of blood.

Wounded rhinos will be likely to attack without provocation. The wounding may not be the result of man: rhino bulls injured in fights over territory or during the mating season will charge, and females who may have been hurt during mating are also unpredictable. If a rhino's flank wounds are annoying him, this may also be a cause for ill-temper. Quite often, whereas an ordinary rhino may charge and then run off, a wounded rhino may be quite persistent in its attacking, returning again and again to attempt contact. I have heard of a wounded rhino identifying the tree in which a man was perching, seeking over and over again to dislodge the intended victim by butting the tree, hooking the trunk with its horn and heaving to and fro and even leaning against the trunk to try to bulldoze the tree flat.

Wounded or whole, it is generally accepted that the black rhino is the more dangerous of the two African species. The following newspaper article more than amply shows that rhinos are not to be toyed with, that they must be respected and regarded with considerable caution.

White Woman Charged by Two Rhinos
Terrible Experience in Rift Valley
Partially Scalped
Carried Four Miles by Camp Natives

Mrs Bailey, wife of Mr G.L. Bailey, of "Sterndale", Nairobi, is an inmate of Nairobi European Hospital after being the victim of an experience which comes within the lives of few women. She owes the fact that she is still alive to some miraculous intervention or accident of which she is quite unaware.

While hunting in Suswa, the mountain which rises above the Great Rift Valley and is one of the breasts of the Queen of Sheba in the mythology and ancient history of Africa, she was charged by two rhinoceroses and very seriously injured.

This is the thrilling story of her adventure:

Mr and Mrs Bailey were on safari and had established their camp near Suswa for a week. On the night before the accident they had been sitting up for lions, and Mrs Bailey caught a chill. On the following day she decided she would not go far and she intended to spend an uneventful day hunting around the camp for reedbuck with a small rifle. Mr Bailey departed with a gun-bearer to seek game on the plains and Mrs Bailey, with another bearer and a second native, decided to climb Suswa. She found no sign of reedbuck and set out to return to camp. . . .

On the way home she discovered fresh tracks of rhino and suddenly came upon two of the animals lying down under a tree in more or less open ground. She hurried to camp and brought her husband's double .470 rifle and the natives back to the spot. When she arrived she found that the two animals had changed their position and were resting under a thick bush.

Mrs Bailey crept slowly forward until she was well within forty yards. The rhinos were in such a position that one was practically covering the outline of its companion, and she supposed they were an old rhino and a full-grown youngster. The latter was nearest to her and she fired at the rhino on the farther side, choosing as a mark an exposed shoulder to get a heart shot.

The next thing she knew was that they both rose to their feet and rushed through the bush at her, charging side by side. Mrs Bailey's one and only thought was that the end of her life had arrived, and she had no time to turn about or fire a second time.

One of the animals caught her with its horn on her side; the horn travelled right up her body and tore away the whole of the scalp on that side. She was thrown high into the air among the trees, and when she came down the rhino trod upon her as she lay on the ground. . . .

Both native gun-bearers stood the strain well. They were experienced men, and they kept their ground. As soon as opportunity offered they lifted the injured woman up – her face streaming blood – and when she regained her feet, she discovered that one of the rhinos was rapidly returning. The natives dragged Mrs Bailey into a dry water gully, and the gun-bearer drove the animal off with rifle fire. Then they set out to carry Mrs Bailey four miles to camp and luckily met another party of camp porters who had been in the same locality for the camp water supply. Among them they brought her down, quite unconscious, and one native hurried on ahead to inform Mr Bailey who met the party bringing his injured wife about a mile from camp. . . .

Mr Bailey immediately placed her in his car and took her to Naivasha where the District Commissioner called in a doctor. Mrs Bailey was removed to the farm and given emergency attention, after which the doctor ordered her removal to Nairobi hospital.

Dr Jewell, on examination, found that the skull was intact, but Mrs Bailey will require the most careful attention for some time before she regains strength after the terrifying experience. She is now progressing slowly but steadily.

It is believed that one of the rhinoceroses has been shot, and Mr Bailey is returning to Suswa in search of the other.

It is somewhat ironic to note how the newspaper lists the incident as an accident: it was clearly an error of judgment on the part of Mrs Bailey. And, in the time-honoured tradition of hunting, the animals which had exhibited the effrontery to attack a human were slaughtered.

What the woman had most likely come upon was a loose alliance of two black rhinos, the older one living its normal solitary existence, the younger one having temporarily joined up with it on being ousted by its mother on the arrival of a new calf. It would have been prudent to have let sleeping rhinos lie: even if the first rhino had been killed outright, the chances of the second charging under the circumstances were better than odds on. As it was, both rhinos were suddenly frightened and reacted predictably. The possibility of Mrs Bailey being able to kill both animals was beyond calculation and the chance of her hitting the second, in mid-charge, slim. Furthermore, she had not covered her escape by positioning herself near a handy tree. The whole episode indicates a gross ignorance of rhinos and basic bushcraft.

Not all rhino stories are, however, so indicative of the animal's purported ferocity. It is (like most wild creatures) usually a docile beast unless aroused by fear, hunger or pain.

J.A. Hunter, one of the most famous and widely-respected of white hunters, reported an incident which showed a black rhino not only to be far from bellicose but also in possession of a sense of fun, if not humour. Hunter was in the bush with an Indian doctor and secretary to a famous rajah. Whilst hunting a buffalo on foot in

Kenya, they came upon a black rhino bull which trotted out of a thicket towards the doctor.

The animal had evidently been disturbed by the stampeding buffalo and was looking for a quieter spot. If the doctor had stood still, all would have been well, but instead he screamed and raced for the startled secretary, apparently hoping the rhino would take off in pursuit of the other man. The secretary quickly realised what was happening and made for the nearest tree. He flattened himself against the stem like a poster and yelled 'Go away! Go 'way!' to the frantic doctor.

The rhino had stopped for a moment when the doctor began to run. Then he started after him, making rooting motions in the air with his horn. The doctor put up a fine sprint, for his heart was in it, but the rhino easily overtook him. The doctor was in line with the rhino so I could not shoot but I soon saw that the beast was not making a serious charge. There is always some degree of safety in a rhino's coming unexpectedly on a man instead of vice versa for the beast is not unduly alarmed. The doctor ran through the thorn trees screaming 'Help!' while the rhino galloped behind, encouraging his victim to fresh efforts by an occasional jab of his horn. As the doctor became so weak that he could only stagger, the rhino slowed down to a trot, still keeping behind him. I became so interested in this performance that I forgot all about shooting the bull and watched with curiosity while the rhino chivvied the man through the scrub. At last, tiring of the sport, the rhino trotted off and the doctor returned to us, sweating and exhausted. His first earnest words were, 'I have had much troubles.'

Sadly, the chances of encountering a rhino in the area in which the doctor had his troubles and the Baileys were hunting, the Kedong Valley on the other side of the Ngong Hills from Nairobi, is now exceedingly remote. Poaching, agricultural encroachment and habitat destruction have done for them all.

HUNTERS AND RHINOS

Hunting and the rhino have been inextricably linked for
centuries and no book about the African rhino can ignore
this fact. The rhino, being the second largest land mammal, has inevitably been considered a worthwhile trophy. It is
difficult to track, hard to shoot and, potentially at any rate, dangerous. The rhino, especially the thicket-dwelling black rhino, tests a
hunter to his limits.

I can think of nothing more repugnant than killing a rhino – or
any other animal, come to that – 'for fun'. The gratuitous rhino-
hunter fits into the same category as the fox-hunter, covered so
ironically by that most famous of Shavian dicta 'the unspeakable in
pursuit of the uneatable'.

At this point, I feel I should state how I regard hunting, and big
game hunting in particular.

When I was a young teenager, in the days of Rhino Road, I shot
game. Of course, I never aspired to the Big Five but I did shoot
small animals – birds, hares, dik-dik and small antelope. The thrill
of this experience for me was the tracking, not the killing. In order
to hunt successfully, I had to learn to stalk, for wild animals are
clever and have their instincts honed almost to telepathic fineness by
aeons of experience. I was merely a schoolboy who normally lived
in a city and was very much a novice.

Other boys with whom I attended school in Nairobi were born
and bred white Kenyans: in many instances, their families lived or
farmed in the bush and made their livelihood from it. They were
attuned to a life in the wild, but I was more or less alien to this: my
father was a colonial civil servant.

Gradually, I learned to track, to understand the signs of bent
twigs and a flattened tussock of grass. I could tell how old spoor

was by the nap on the sand, how fresh a pellet of dung was and what animal had made it, how much at danger (or not) was my predicament.

My first tracking forays took place in the Langata Forest, between Nairobi and Karen, the former home of Karen Blixen. I began by hunting butterflies but was alarmed so often by a sudden rustle or a low grunt in the undergrowth it was inevitable that I should have to discover what these creatures were, if only for my own peace of mind.

From Langata, I graduated to countryside to the north-east of Thika, out towards the Ithanga Hills, in the area made famous by Elspeth Huxley[1]. I seldom shot for food (save the odd guinea-fowl), almost always for sport. Gradually, however, I found the appeal of shooting to be waning. As I was no taxidermist (although I had a go once or twice with messy, abhorrent results)– there seemed little point in killing an animal in order to see it lying dead.

It was then that I came upon the writings of Jim Corbett[2]. He was an Englishman born and bred in India although he retired to and died in Nyeri, near Mount Kenya in 1955. He was one of the seminal modern conservationists, a man of boundless courage, humanity and with an incredible knowledge of jungle lore. He too had been a hunter and later changed his ways, shooting only for the pot and to rid the Himalayan foothills of their worst scourge – man-eating tigers and leopards.

I devoured his stories and have never lost the deep interest and concern for nature which they aroused in me.

Today, when the chance affords itself, I still shoot but only for the pot and only animals which I know are still abundant and, more importantly, are going to remain so in the distant future. I have taken part in an antelope cull in recent years but have otherwise restricted my shooting to pigeons and the like in English fields.

For me, the intense and rewarding enjoyment, the peril, the thrill and the risk is to be found in tracking. And I do want trophies, not to show my machismo and skill but the wonders of the natural world to others. My trophies now are printed on high-grade photographic paper and hang in my home. Unlike mounted heads or cured skins, they do not deteriorate, go shabby and bald, smell musty and eventually become consigned to the dustbin.

I do have some game products in my study and I am not ashamed of these: a Kenyan leopard skin shot in 1928 and rescued from the floor of a junk shop, and a zebra-skin native drum circa 1955 purchased in a jumble sale. The other items were obtained without the animal dying other than by natural causes – two hippo's incisors taken from a skull dredged from a river, a buffalo's vertebra I obtained shortly after the lion had finished sucking the taste out, a dung-beetle mud-ball from which I watched a spotted hyena eat the large and juicy grub . . . These are just as much a trophy to me as any stuffed pelt: they bring back to me memories of certain days and events in the company of wild animals.

I believe I am somewhat more mature now than to need to kill an animal to illustrate my manhood. To me, the hunter after sport trophies is an immature being for whom killing is a vicarious gratification of primeval urges which he (or she) should be more capable of controlling and suppressing.

Having said this, I do admire some of the big-game hunters of old. They did not live in a world such as the present day: game was plentiful, wild places common and not under threat. For them, different mores and rules governed their lives and I cannot condemn out of hand all of them for their behaviour. Furthermore, they did not just kill animals as do modern hunters, whom I do condemn.

Unlike the majority of today's hunters who fly in by jet, kill without any real feeling for their target animals, or with little more than a passing understanding or a transient appreciation of the habitat and its problems, and who return home to boast of their prowess, the old hunters understood and respected their quarry. They were often serious naturalists and their knowledge and expertise contributed a great deal towards our understanding of different species, habitat change and game management. They despised the hunters who shot from vehicles, such 'hunting' still going on today in some places: the language they would use in speaking of those who in recent years have shot from helicopters could not be printed.

These old-time hunters were also men of vision: Corbett foresaw the demise of the tiger in India through deforestation just as Charles Cottar simultaneously predicted the downfall of the rhino through intensified agriculture and subsequent loss of habitat. Even the first Boer settlers in Cape Province saw the need to curb their hunting. As early as 1657 and again in 1684, the Dutch settlers restricted each farmer to the killing of one rhino, one hippo and one eland per annum.

And so I feel a few extracts of hunters' tales of rhinos are justified . . .

Some of the early hunters of rhinos were prodigal in their shooting of the species. For this they cannot necessarily be criticised: by the standard of their times they were behaving normally, for rhinos were in considerable abundance and suitable natural habitat covered more than seventy per cent of sub-Saharan Africa. Today, that area has been trimmed to less than ten per cent.

In 1836, on what might be called the first-ever safari, organised by Sir William Cornwallis Harris and his companion, William Richardson, the latter narrowly escaped death when a rhino he had wounded charged his horse. Despite Richardson's galloping his horse away, the rhino kept up with it and Richardson only avoided being killed by shooting the rhino with the barrel of his rifle in its mouth. As the rhino fell, the gun was wrenched from Richardson's hands and damaged beyond repair. This rhino was in many ways lucky. The weapons used for hunting were muzzle-loaders firing ball shot (like a musket ball), not a bullet in the modern sense: Harris records having to hit a rhino twenty-seven times before it fell.

Another nineteenth-century hunter, an eccentric Scotsman called Roualeyn Gordon Cumming, hunted big game with a pack of dogs: this was not unknown well into the twentieth century and I know of one person who hunted lion with a pack of South African Ridgebacks in Kenya as recently as the late 1940s. However Cumming, who once shot seven rhinos in a day and noted in his diary the shrill cry they uttered as they died, did not use his dogs on rhinos because they could not bring a rhino to bay. Faced with the dogs, the rhinos fled: no doubt thoughts of hyenas hunting young rhinos in a pack prompted this flight.

Some hunters exhibited a distinct lack of respect towards the rhinos which they killed. I find this abhorrent. No one has the right to belittle a creature.

In his as-yet unpublished memoirs, Syd Downey, one of the early twentieth-century shooting safari operators writes[3]:

In the early 1950s Kris Aschan and I took a large safari party to Tanganyika. One well-known member of this party was Lauritz

97

Melchior the Wagnerian opera singer. Lauritz had a passion for cards, which often took preference over all other activities including meals.

We were camped in what is now the Lake Manyara National Park; the quarry was rhino of which there were many at that time. Lauritz easily obtained his trophy, and the professional photographer, hired by the party, was taking the usual set of pictures – Lauritz with his rhino.

Finally the photographer said: 'Now, Mr Melchior, there is just one more picture I must have,' and in answer to the query which followed he said: 'I want a shot of you playing cards on the rhino's back.'

One wonders why Melchior went on safari if his all-abiding interest was so distant from that of appreciating – even shooting – wildlife. But such were the foibles and attitudes of a good many wealthy or celebrity safari-goers. It was not the wildlife they went for, or the experience of Africa, or the wonderment of wilderness: they went because to go on safari was fashionable, was *de rigueur*. And killing a rhino – or a lion or an elephant – was also the 'done thing'.

Some early safari clients did show respect for their quarry, but it was frequently a patronising regard borne out of their being out of touch with the wildlife of Africa and the etiquette of living with nature. George Eastman, the founder of Kodak, wrote[4] of a rhino he killed in Kenya in August 1926:

. . . the third, a cow with a yearling calf, got our scent at about 150 yards and suddenly turned down the slope and charged us full tilt. I got off Tsetse [Eastman's horse], grabbed my gun and we all stood ready. We thought at first we could frighten her off without making any shooting noise and all began to yell, but on she came with her calf following. At thirty-five yards (afterwards measured) Pat thought she was near enough and gave her a shot from his .465. It grazed her front horn and entered her left shoulder. It did not stop her, however, and as I was next I put a 470 in the center of her right shoulder, and she dropped dead twenty-six yards from where we stood. The bullet had passed through her heart. In the meantime the calf had come up and stopped in front of its dead mother. It looked around and saw a lunch basket and one of my folding camp chairs that a couple of porters had dropped when they went up a tree. With a rush it caught the chair and gave it a vicious throw over its head. Then it started for Audley and me, and we each gave it a shot (joined by Saasita with the Mannlicher as he thought bwana Eastman was in for it), whereupon it ran off on three legs squealing. After examining the dead mother, Pat took the Mannlicher and went off a couple of hundred yards and put out of its misery the young one, which had a broken shoulder and was bleeding at the mouth from a shot through the lungs. When it was all over we were more than thankful than ever that the rhino of the day before had behaved like a gentleman.

Like a gentleman, indeed! I am quite sure it would have done and it is a pity Eastman could not follow its example by refraining from killing a cow with a calf. No professional white hunter would have behaved so: he would have stayed on his horse and ridden it away.

The arrogance of hunters – the client hunter, not the professional – is to me almost as obscene as their random killing.

For most white hunters, respect was a vitally important part of their relationship with their quarry. It was not accepted to kill at random and many white hunters privately despised their clients who would go trigger-happy when surrounded by vast quantities of game. This blasé attitude most often came to the fore when hunting the Big Five and, especially, elephant and rhino.

For others – like J.A. Hunter – the killing of rhinos was their job. J.A. Hunter was employed by the government of Kenya – between 1946 and 1950 – to shoot black rhino in the defence of agriculture. He wrote[5] quite straightforwardly about shooting a rhino:

Rhinos are a special problem. Not much sense in trying to stand and stare them out, for if they know you're there they're usually charging you madly. And you want to make sure you shoot them – and shoot to kill – before they get closer than five yards – otherwise the impetus of the charging body (even though the rhino is technically dead) will topple you over and crush you. I have heard people talk of stepping aside from the oncoming bodies of rhino they have just shot, but have never seen it done.

It is not easy to stalk rhinos to their resting places, even if the wind is in the right direction and one is absolutely silent in approaching. They are peculiarly sensitive to the presence of man and appear restless even though they may not be directly aware that you are watching them. Flies, buzzing ahead of the hunter in outrider clouds, are partly responsible for raising the alarm, and there are also the rhino-birds – feathered spies whose mission in life is to utter loud chir-chir warning cries as they fly across the bushland and observe dangerous interlopers.

I remember once stalking a trio of rhinos which had been doing considerable harm in a eucalyptus plantation at the foot of the Aberdare mountains, uprooting the trees with their horns and eating the top most succulent shoots. I'd followed them from their night raid on the plantation to their daytime 'lie-up' in the nearby forest – a basin-shaped hollow surrounded by difficult tall greenery which made vision impossible. I could only follow their trail, foot by foot.

This I did for about an hour, having sent my native bearer home because his footsteps had been far from noiseless and I was very anxious to avoid giving the rhinos ahead of me any warning. Coping with a charging rhino in this thick bush wouldn't be all that easy; I wanted to shoot to kill without them being aware of my presence if possible.

Such wind as there was was in my favour and my approach was absolutely noiseless – that I can swear to. But when I came to the hollow and peered through the tall grass and brush to see the three rhinos lying there in a huddle, rather as pigs do in a sty, I could see that they already knew of my presence. They were beginning to become restless, turning their heads uneasily towards me and preparing to attack. A cloud of flies hovered angrily buzzing above the trio and I remembered hearing the buzzing of flies quite near to me a few minutes earlier. So it may be that flies transmit either a secret warning or bear on themselves the smell of approaching man.

In that particular incident, by the way, the rhinos lost no time in translating their uneasiness into terms of action. They came charging through the undergrowth straight at me, each trying to get ahead of the others. I fired my .500 D/B Express at the face of the middle attacker. The shot hit her between eye and ear and she dropped dead instantly, her body raising a great cloud of dust as it hit the ground. The other two leapt from the side of their dead companion with the agility of cats – unbelievable in view of their great weight and ponderous bodies – turned and were gone almost before I had time to realise that I was out of danger.

Even though I once carried out the greatest rhino drive of all time – in the Makueni district, to make way for a post-war settlement of Wakamba – I have never ceased to be especially cautious in tracking rhino because of their extra-sensory perception. On only one occasion in my life have I ever got really close to a rhino without his knowledge and that time I was so close that I actually hung my stetson hat on his horn. But he was an oldish bull and he was fast asleep. It was quite an occasion, though; for in a moment or two he detected something wrong, rose puffing and snorting from his rest and went charging off with the stetson still poised on his horn.

Exit rhino to the sound of gales of laughter – mine and my native bearers', who stood holding their sides and rocking with mirth at the droll sight, even though a moment before they had been warning me – with justifiable horror – not to attempt to do such a mad thing.

Elsewhere in his book, which is one of the most important autobiographies[6] by any twentieth-century white hunter/conservationist and essential reading for anyone who wishes to understand the mentality and life of the genuine hunter, Hunter relates another incident with rhinos. It took place whilst he was not on safari going after wild animals but in pursuit of ruthless, organised Ethiopian game poachers:

I accelerated a bit as I went down the slope and crossed the stream with hardly a splash. Beyond, the path twisted upwards between acacias and dense thorn; and it was as I rounded a bend that I saw the rhinos – four of them huddled together like hippos directly in my path glaring at me angrily.

I stopped the truck and got down. Any other time rhinos would have ambled off at the sight of a truck. These, however, decided to stand their ground. They continued to glare at me as I got out of the vehicle. Then two of them got up and lumbered off into the bush. The other two puffed and snorted, then rose and moved belligerently towards me. I didn't like the look of them at all – especially as I was now standing between them and the truck, which was blocking my own escape route.

The leading rhino – a large cow with particularly long horns –
now decided to charge. She came at me pell-mell, head down. At
about fifteen yards I fired the right-hand barrel of my D/B .500
and she collapsed dead. Instantly the bull followed, came to the
dead body of his mate and attempted to jump over it. At the same
time the two beasts that had wandered off emerged from the bush
– I could see them out of the corner of my eye, tossing their heads
angrily at the smell of death and preparing an attack. But there
was no time to consider them. The charging bull had already
clambered over the obstructing body and was coming for me.
The sandy dust rose in a cloud, obscuring my vision; but without
aiming properly I scored a lucky shot between the eye and the
base of the ear and the beast toppled over sideways. The remaining two rhinos were altogether beyond me. They were coming
for me diagonally, both chambers of my rifle were empty and
there was no time to reload. I made a hopeless effort at opening
the breech, but by then they were on top of me. The whole of
Africa seemed at that moment confined to the narrow space
between the trees of a thicket – a small world filled with pande-
monium, dust, dappling sunlight and fear.

No: perhaps not fear on this occasion. There was really no time
to be fearful and nothing to do except hurl myself sideways on to
the dead body of the bull rhino, which by its impetus had skidded
almost to my feet, and cling on to its horn as I sprawled across
the great head and neck.

The two charging beasts now collided sideways as they met on
precisely the spot where I'd been standing a second before. The
thud of their collision made the earth shake. One of them was so
winded that I caught the great wheezing blast of breath he snorted
out. It was exactly like human halitosis smelt through an olfactory amplifier. If I hadn't been pretty well knocked out by my
strategical tumble I might have felt like swooning with the over-
powering stench.

But this was no occasion for swooning. The two rhinos had
winded each other to such an extent that they were bewildered
and in trying to regain their balance and turn to meet their mutual
enemy – me – one of them fell ponderously on to its side while
the other was again knocked off its balance and fell too. For a few
seconds there was a whirling mass of legs, flanks and horns, a
great bellowing and violent scattering of dust and clods of earth

102

and bits of foliage. Once the whirling beasts lashed out so close to me that I felt a sickening thud on the neck of the dead rhino against whose head I was crouched. I took advantage of the turmoil to risk grabbing at my rifle, which had fallen a few feet away as I leapt out of the path of the charging beasts. In doing so I left myself totally unprotected, for I had to leave the shelter of the dead body and dive almost into the middle of the mêlée. But I got hold of it somehow and loaded it just as the two rhinos regained their balance. As luck would have it, their confusion was now so great that they went charging through the thicket away from me. I stood for a few minutes with my rifle at the ready, watching the screen of dust settle and hearing the great bodies trampling murderously through the bush.

Well, I was out of immediate danger – incidentally one of the trickiest bits of immediate danger I'd ever been in – but my path through the wood was now inconveniently blocked by the bodies of the two dead rhinos. There was no room to turn the truck; my only course was to reverse all the way back along the path and out of the wood, then to regain the road and start all over again. This I did, slowly and with considerable apprehension, for I was both trying to guide the truck along a four-foot wide twisting path by reference to the view in the driving mirror and at the same time half expecting to have to deal with the two angry beasts which might at any moment decide to come charging out of the bush. Nothing spectacular happened, however. The only delay was when I got the truck jammed between two trees and had to get out and use a matchet to free the mudguard. I even managed to cross the little stream in reverse without getting stuck. But just as I'd completed that rather tricky bit of driving and was well up the slope on the farther side I saw to my amazement that yet another rhino had stepped from the bush and was blocking my path.

This time I paused only a second to think. There was no point at all in shooting the beast where it stood, since I should then have the path blocked at both ends with bodies of dead rhinos and would be unable to get the truck out at all. My only hope was to get the rhino out of the way by threat or noise. I have often found that rhinos will dash off if they hear the sound of a police whistle; and this I now tried, blowing shrill blasts with all the power of my lungs.

103

The rhino continue to stand there, eyeing me truculently the while he contemptuously let fall a great steaming heap of excrement which he immediately began to scatter with his hind legs, as a dog does. But he wouldn't budge even when I'd blown myself nearly blue in the face. Obstinate and moody as all his race, he had simply decided to stand there and challenge me.

Well, if whistle-blowing wouldn't move him perhaps the threat of impact would. I let in the clutch and accelerated. The engine roared because of the low reverse gear. I was trying to dodge trees and speed up at the same time. But even the threat of being charged by a heavy truck wouldn't move my enemy. In fact, at the moment when I was perhaps thirty yards from him he decided that the best method of defence was attack, took a few final kicks at the ground beneath his back legs, and came charging down the path towards me.

This is it, I thought, the truck's going to be a pretty wreck after he's gone to work on it. Even so, I still wouldn't risk a shot at him – I suppose because there was always a chance that he'd change direction at the last minute, whereas if I killed him he couldn't fall anywhere but in my path.

He didn't change direction, though: he came full tilt in a cloud of dust until we couldn't have been more than ten yards apart. Then both he and I skidded to a standstill. I could see his great head rearing and snorting as the dust cleared. Then he came ponderously on towards the back of the truck. I thought he'd realised he was defeated and might now crash off into the bush; but oh no! of course he wasn't defeated, and of course he was as obstinate as ever. But he had a sense of humour. I watched him stroll up to the tailboard, lower his head and lift the back of the lorry with his horn. Three times he raised and bumped it to the ground. Then, seemingly, the tip of his horn, which must have become embedded in the woodwork, broke off and the whole weight of the lorry crashed down on his snout. Even his thick skin couldn't take such treatment, and, giving a roar of pain, he suddenly turned and crashed off through the bush.

Hunter's attitude was human and humane. He was not – as was and is the case with the vast majority of professional hunters – a cruel and bloodthirsty man but a person with a considerable feeling for wildlife. The bloodthirsty ones were the clients.

Of these, two spring most immediately to mind. The first is Theodore Roosevelt who went on safari with his son, Kermit, in 1909. Financed by Andrew Carnegie at a cost of US$75,000 (at modern values about $1.2 million) and the Smithsonian Institute, it was purportedly a scientific safari, but Roosevelt, who was an avid animal killer, took great delight in bagging 512 animals including eleven elephants, twenty rhinos and seventeen lions. With accompanying naturalists, who no doubt gave the safari a degree of respectability, the total number of animals sent back to the USA in the name of science was nearly 5000 mammals, 4000 birds and 2000 reptiles.

He later defended criticism of his excessive shooting by saying it was for scientific purposes and, indeed, many of his animals were so used and some stand today stuffed in the Smithsonian Institute in Washington DC. The truth was that Roosevelt shot for what he himself termed 'the strong eager pleasure of it' and for this he was quietly despised. Roosevelt often shot badly, from too great a distance and many of his 'kills' were actually finished off by professional white hunters.

Where the rhino was concerned, he was callous, not a hunter but an executioner. Despite claiming to be a hunter-conservationist, Roosevelt killed nine northern white rhinos in the Lado Enclave – including four cows and a calf, and wounded two calves – knowing full well as he did so that the white rhino was virtually extinct in southern Africa and on the verge of disappearing in the region in which he was hunting.

This was reprehensible and showed the bad side of hunting, that the rules were sometimes bent in the name of sheer profit, cruel and self-indulgent sport and supposed 'scientific' progress.

Another despicable hunter was the novelist Ernest Hemingway.

When he first went on safari in 1933, Hemingway was in his prime, a successful and famous (even notorious) novelist, a man of action but with a grossly inflated opinion of himself. A more than competent shot, he entered wholeheartedly into the spirit of the safari and revelled in the excitement, thrill and sense of power stalking and shooting gave him. However, he also possessed a streak of intense cruelty and he shot not only for the pot, for sport and for a trophy but also to see the pain he could inflict. He liked shooting baboons because they looked like men as they fell, staggered and died: he despised the hyena, ignorant of its fascinating

105

natural history, and once enjoyed the sight of one, which he had hit in the belly, snapping at its wound until it finally tore out its own entrails and ate them.

For Hemingway, the safari was a means of proving his manhood, and all his shooting became a form of competition between himself and his peers: on his first safari, Archibald MacLeish, the American poet, declined to accompany him knowing that this would be the case – that the animals would die vicariously to support Hemingway's sense of machismo. For Hemingway, the safari gave him the opportunity to indulge himself in his primitive drives, for which he was quietly rebuked by the white hunter organising the safari, Philip Percival. Percival hunted by the rules, refusing to allow anything to be killed except that which they were specifically after: there was, as Hemingway put it himself, no 'killing on the side, no ornamental killing'. For Hemingway, all killing was an ornament upon the statue of his grandiose ego.

The first black rhino Hemingway saw was spotted in what is today the Lake Manyara National Park on the Kenya-Tanzania border near Mount Kilimanjaro. He wrote of seeing it 'red-coloured in the sun, moving with a quick water-bug-like motion'. Three other rhinos came into view along an edge of woodland, and Hemingway, watching through binoculars, saw two of them fighting. He later killed his first rhino at the considerable range of over 250 metres, a shot that was as accurate as it was remarkable. Hemingway's pride at this shot, and the quality of the trophy, was deflated when he discovered his hunting companion had killed a far bigger animal earlier the same day. He was consumed with jealousy for the other's finer trophy: the rhino had died to satisfy his vanity and had failed so to do.

As for many men, Hemingway's killing of big game was merely an aspect of his seeking to establish his virility, prove his manliness and somehow increase his self-esteem. Such hunting is, for me, a sign of human weakness and somewhat puerile. I remember once being told by Norman Carr, the famous conservationist who first 'lived' with wild lions as, later, George and Joy Adamson were to do, that hunting big game is an indication of an individual's immaturity and lack of self-confidence and esteem: I believe he was being utterly astute in this opinion.

It follows, therefore, that the bigger the target animal – and, consequently, the greater the potential danger one might be in from it – the higher will be the score of esteem points to be gained from killing it. For this reason, the black rhino with its unpredictable charge and apparent short temper has always been a sought-after trophy.

In 1953, Hemingway went on his last safari. His shooting abilities had faded, his health was ruined by alcohol: he shaved his head, rubbed red mud into his clothes like a Masai *moran* (or warrior), hunted small game with a spear, with limited success, and had an affair with a young Wakamba woman. He claimed as his own several kills made by another hunter on the safari. Percival told Hemingway the whole safari had been a disgrace.

Fortunately, clients who behaved in this fashion were not the norm. For example, when shooting on safari, the Prince of Wales (later King Edward VIII), devoutly obeyed all the rules: it was when taking photographs that he was somewhat less than obedient. A keen photographer, the prince wanted a picture of a charging rhino during his 1930 safari in Kenya: he also wanted to take the photo from on foot and not from within the safety of a safari vehicle. Denys Finch Hatton was the white hunter in charge of the safari and, with the help of Archie Ritchie, later to be the influential Chief Game Warden for the country, manoeuvred a black rhino into position. It dutifully charged, drawing closer and closer to the heir to the English throne. At last, not daring to take any further risk with his client's life, Finch Hatton brought the animal down stone dead with a single frontal shot. It fell within twenty feet of the camera. The prince, however, was furious: he wanted the rhino to fill the complete frame of his viewfinder before pressing the shutter. He was also more than saddened at what he considered the unnecessary killing: yet, had the hunter not acted, the prince would have suffered the same fate that Charles Cottar did a decade later.

Not all hunting stories relate to the shooting of rhinos. As cameras – in particular ciné-cameras – developed, so did rhino hunters turn from merely killing to shooting with film. Osa and Martin Johnson were among the early film- and bullet-shooters, the latter not only as a last resort in self-defence but also to produce a thrilling effect, as has been mentioned. They were an American couple who became famous as world explorers, but it was in East Africa that they achieved that which made them most famous but not always popular. They claimed that they discovered Lake Paradise but in fact white hunters had been there before them: Cottar had been the first white man to visit the place.

Osa, who was besotted with Africa and African wildlife, and became a competent if amateurish and unscientific naturalist, wrote[7] of many rhino encounters, one of which involved film footage and a dead animal:

> At the water holes at night we were always sure of at least one good rhino fight. They locked horns at the slightest provocation, or for no reason at all, and gored each other terribly. Nine out of ten rhino wear huge open wounds or scars from these fights. Some of the gashes are as large as dinner-plates, and I am sure these must contribute to the animal's ugly disposition.
>
> Usually the fight was over a female. And the females seemed to enjoy the rows, even to encourage them. A coy two-ton lady would rub against the side of one of the big fellows and trot around in a silly way, then go over and rub noses with the other male. Then the trouble would start. The males would paw the ground, race at each other, clinch and whirl around in circles, snorting like locomotives. Sometimes a fight would last the entire night and completely wear us out watching it.
>
> Trying to get flashlights of one of these encounters, Martin and I set up an elaborate arrangement of cameras at a water hole and secreted ourselves in a thornbush blind. Soon a rhino and his mate appeared, sniffed around for a while and then gave our cameras a wide berth, although the wind was right and they should not have got our scent. They went off to the edge of the pool. In a few minutes another male appeared and in no time at all a fight was on, completely out of range of our cameras.
>
> The fight ended abruptly after about twenty minutes, and the rhinos came back and went off up the trail down which they had come. But they met other rhino who were coming down to water. Instead of fighting the newcomers, all stopped and seemed to have a sort of conference, then the new arrivals came down the trail and skirted our blind and cameras, just as the others had done. They also stormed around for a time and went off without giving us a picture. We concluded that the first rhinos had somehow warned the others and that perhaps there was some real fraternity among them after all.

'Rhinos never attack man unless they are provoked,' Blaney had once said. Therefore I was very amused when Blaney was charged by a rhino one day as he drove serenely along in a car, with no intention of provoking anything. Even though he shot into the air and finally shot the rhino on the horn to divert him, the beast tore into Blaney's car and ruined the radiator.

'Must have been something wrong with that one,' remarked Blaney, very perplexed.

We never shot rhino unless we had no other choice. Our business was to get pictures, and when a rhino did charge the cameras we shot into the ground, into the air and all around him, trying to scare him off. Sometimes I would shoot one at the base of the horn with a solid-nosed bullet which would ricochet off and not wound the animal, but would give him a good headache for a couple of hours. Frequently the rhino could not be frightened. We learned from long experience to tell when he wasn't bluffing and meant business. Then it became a question of his life or ours.

In addition to our feeling against killing, it cost us fifty dollars to shoot each rhino, and several times that amount for each elephant; so using our lungs or firing in the air to scare them off was an economy.

At Lake Paradise one afternoon we were photographing a mother rhino and her baby. This is always dangerous, because any mother animal with a baby is jittery and will charge on sight, and the rhino is particularly suspicious.

Martin had risen from the ferns in which we were concealed and was cranking the camera. The baby spied us, ran under its mother, then out again, and the mother, now thoroughly alarmed, began looking for us.

'Look!' I whispered suddenly.

Martin turned quicker than a shot. There, walking straight for us, was a big bull rhino, his head lowered and his two horns aimed straight at the camera.

I grabbed my .465 elephant gun.

'See if you can turn him,' Martin shouted.

I shot over his back, screamed, shot at his horn. On he came.

I knew Martin was making a good film of the rhino, and probably thought this was one of those familiar false alarms. I didn't think so, however, and I was right. The rhino stopped, snorted and charged. At twenty-five feet I aimed and shot for the brain. The great brute fell.

It was not all one-sided. The animals had their various revenges upon the hunters. The noun nonchalantly used to describe these incidents is a 'hammering' and many hunters or safari people have in their time been 'hammered' by a buffalo, an elephant – or a rhino: they too have had their fair share of retribution against the human race and those who would kill them.

William Cotton Oswell was charged by a white rhino whilst on horseback. The rhino gored and killed the horse as both rider and mount were tossed into the air. Cotton Oswell lost a part of his scalp. On another occasion, whilst hunting rhino on foot, he mis-judged the animals' behaviour and was charged. He decided he was unable to fell the oncoming animals and so took to his heels, weaving and jinking to throw them off. This tactic failed and one of the rhinos gored him in the thigh. He shot the animal at point-blank range just as it lifted him off the ground. When he came round, Cotton Oswell could feel his thigh-bone exposed in the wound on his leg. It took him over a month to recover and he was exceedingly lucky: such a wound usually turned gangrenous in those days of primitive medicine.

The mother of one of Kenya's most renowned modern white hunters, Tony Seth-Smith, was hunting on Suswa Mountain in the Rift Valley – close to the same area where Mrs Bailey was charged – when she was charged, also by two black rhinos. She wounded one with her rifle, stopping it but the second animal reached her and rammed its horn up the side of her body, taking her scalp off and tossing her. The rhino then stomped on her and broke a number of her ribs. She succeeded in killing the rhino, made her way down the mountain, crossed the Rift Valley floor to the Nairobi-Nakuru rail-way line, stopped a train and remained conscious until she arrived at the hospital in Nairobi. Her son has the rhino's horn mounted in his house to this day: his mother's scalp still hangs from it.

Of course, it was not just European hunters who were taken by rhinos and not all of those attacked survived. Hunter records the story[8] of a native scout he knew in Kenya:

Detei was a simple, God-fearing soul and I found his charm endearing. He was typical of his tribe in his simplicity and loyalty

110

and would always go out of his way to help me in any difficulties I encountered.

When he heard that three rhinos had become a source of danger to the people of a tiny village ten miles or so from Makindu he came and told me and asked if we could go in pursuit. It seemed that the rhinos had lately been attacking the village women who were going peacefully about their domestic chores – particularly when they were drawing water and carrying it home in gourds. Returning from the streams carrying their gourds they would be quite unable to move quickly and the rhinos would emerge from nearby cover and gore them in their well-proportioned buttocks. This naturally incurred the wrath of women and husbands who now requested protection – and death to the sour-tempered beasts.

Detei and a fellow native scout started off at crack of dawn. Luck came to them early and Detei encountered one of the wanted trio – a mature bull – in a tangled thicket on the outskirts of the village. It was busily chewing sapless thorn when the scouts came upon it and looked up in surprise as Detei levelled his rifle. A second later it dropped dead.

At the sound of the shot a number of tick birds, which had been busily engaged on picking the parasites from the backs of several other rhinos a little distance off, rose in flight. The flurry of birds gave the alarm to a cow and calf rhino which immediately galloped off, heading for the refuge of denser thicket across the plain.

Unperturbed Detei and his fellow scout followed. It was some distance and the ground was hard and dry, but eventually they picked up the spoor and entered the thicket.

The density of the thorn precluded any possibility of good vision and they were forced to stand and peer about them for the quarry. Unhappily the wind had changed and the rhinos had become aware of their pursuers' presence. Immediately the cow rhino charged from a very short distance ahead, and such is their mobility in even the densest scrub that they were upon the two scouts before there was the slightest possibility of taking aim or even raising the rifles.

The second scout was able to jump aside; but Detei was not so fortunate: he was hemmed in by the thorn and could not move quickly enough in any direction. The thundering beast came

111

down upon him, its great foot giving him a powerful blow at the side of the neck, breaking it instantly.

When we found him he was on his knees with his rifle still in his hands. But its barrel was choked with earth; he had not had time to raise it but had fallen forward upon it as the rhino's hoof came down on him.

Detei's was a hunter's destiny and a hunter's death. Brief and unspectacular, unknown and unmarked . . .

Not all hammerings occurred in the distant past. In 1977, the Kenyan white hunter turned wildlife sculptor, Terry Matthews, was badly gored by a black rhino. A decade later, he was again badly wounded by a rhino in Nairobi National Park. A brief account of this[9] shows not only the terrible damage the quick flick of horn might cause but also the courage and generosity of those who love the bush and its residents.

Matthews was accompanying an American film crew on foot in Nairobi National Park, about seventeen km. as the crow flies from the city centre: he was not armed for it is forbidden to carry a firearm into a Kenyan reserve.

As Terry crouched quietly, unarmed, near a female rhinoceros and her calf, one eager photographer, ignoring Terry's instructions, kept standing and pressing forward, camera whirring, twice drawing the rhino's anxious attention. Provoked, the rhinoceros finally charged. The photographer ran past behind Terry. Protecting the film crew ten yards behind him by standing his ground, Terry shouted and threw a stone to deflect the charging rhino as the animal lowered its head, coming in fast.

Weighing one ton or more and capable of thirty miles an hour, black rhinos gallop only when charging. They hit with the impact of a small truck. As Terry stood firm, the long front horn entered the pocket of his shorts, punched into his thigh, tore the lining of his colon, and ripped sixteen inches upwards into his pelvic and abdominal cavity. Only Terry's heavy belt saved him from being torn open as the rhino tossed him ten feet into the air.

The long slender horn missed his spleen, kidneys, major arteries, heart and lungs. Surviving, appreciating his luck, with two ribs and one leg badly broken, Terry complained from his hospital bed that, although he had absorbed sixteen inches of the world's finest aphrodisiac, he had never felt less sexy. Instead of flowers to the hospital, he asked friends to send contributions to the Sheldrick Wildlife Appeal for rhinoceros protection work.

Also, in the 1980s, the then manager of the Nairobi office of Friends of Conservation, Helen de Butts, was gored and seriously injured by a rhino she was seeking to save.

I have often wondered why rhino gorings have so often led to the victim being scalped. The reason is, I assume, that the action of the rhino is to ram its horn upwards. As the black rhino in particular can raise its head a long way, and that the horn can therefore travel a distance of at least the length of a man, it seems probable that the horn can graze along the side of the skull, rather than pierce it. Furthermore, when a human is hit at or below the waist, the top half of the body bends into the blow. As a rhino thumps into a human, the torso will go backwards over what will be a rising, thrusting horn.

The legal hunting of rhino has, without a doubt, contributed significantly to the demise of the animal although the main blame for this, as already stated, has to lie with agricultural encroachment and poaching, the responsibility being more that of the farmer and poacher than the hunter.

The hunters did kill for sport, to obtain trophies to earn an income from rhinos, be that by eradicating them (as J.A. Hunter did) or killing them and selling their product. Yet, at the same time, they also contributed much towards the understanding of rhino natural history, behaviour and physiology. They were instrumental in seeking the protection of rhinos and other game through the establishment of national game reserves, the development of the wildlife tourist industry, the implementation of shooting licences and the controlled utilisation of game.

It is important to remember that many of the safari lodges used today by mass-market tourists were first built by white hunters or their companies. These are the best of their sort, not the package-holiday, Torremolinos-in-The-Bush resorts with swimming pools, tennis courts and TV in the rooms.

I have stayed in a number of these establishments. The best two that I know of are Chinzombo in the South Luangwa National Park in north-eastern Zambia and Cottar's camp just outside the

Masai Mara National Park in western Kenya.

Chinzombo was not built by white hunters but by the Zambian Save the Rhino Trust, in order to give the society a public base in the bush and to encourage foreign tourism, the profits from which went into the trust for the conservation of the local rhino population. The camp stands on (or near to) a place that was a base for white hunters and Arab slavers in the past and was also a camping site on one of Dr Livingstone's missionary expeditions. Erected on the banks of the Luangwa river, a major tributary of the Zambesi river, it consists of two-bed *bandas* with attached simple shower-lavatories. The dining room is an open porch and the very basic bar is on the banks of the river. I have sat at the bar and watched a leopard hunt baboons on the opposite bank and a crocodile take a puku whilst drinking. A wild cat walked into the dining shelter one evening and a hippo eased itself on to the small verandah of my *banda* to scratch its rump on the roof poles.

At Cottar Mara, as the Cottar camp is called – also known as Siana Springs, it stands on the site of Charles Cottar's last camp from which he departed to meet his death by rhino – I have sat around a camp fire and been serenaded (if that is the right word) by the screech of tree hyraxes and had a civet cat walk right past my chair. Baboons barked and scratched themselves on a rough patch of grass which the camp staff played football on and a leopard spent the better part of an hour on the roof of my *banda*, there sawing to another 200 metres off.

Sadly, the days of going on safari in Kenya and seeing rhino have gone. Even sleeping rough in the Masai Mara today will bring no sighting of rhinos unless one is extraordinarily fortunate. (When I slept rough on the banks of the Sand river in the Masai Mara in 1990, the only creatures to visit our little camp were a pair of bat-eared foxes which sniffed at my bald head as I slept and went on their way.)

In the old days, even rhino would come into camp, seemingly unworried by the presence of humans. The white hunter, Blaney Percival, used to tell of a rhino which charged his camp fire one night and stomped it out. The Johnsons' camp was attacked by a rhino which charged an aluminium cooking pan glinting in the bright moonlight. I know of rhinos which have gone through safari camps, tripping over guy ropes and taking tents away wrapped around themselves, later to shred these expensive pieces of equipment in the nearby thorn bush in fits of temper at the canvas trappings.

Many of the game hunters saw it as a part of their lives to protect wildlife. Some went so far as to publish their opinions, not always pleasing their peers. Charles Cottar, for example, foresaw the eventual disappearance of the rhino. As early as the 1930s, he was writing vehemently in defence of the bush and wildlife, criticising unscrupulous or over-zealous hunters and expansionist agriculturalists alike for what they were doing. He did not think the rhino would go as far towards extinction as it has, and he did not foresee that it would be poaching that did for it. Cottar believed loss of habitat would be the cause. Consequently, he fought to preserve wild places just as his great-grandson, Calvin Cottar, does today by actively supporting anti-poaching activities in Kenya, building bush roads and donating staff and vehicles from his safari company to the national wildlife agencies operating in Tsavo East.

Cottar is not alone in this. The international tourist firm, Abercrombie & Kent, one of the founders of which is a Kenya-bred Englishman, puts back into conservation a percentage of earnings from East African tourism and provides its organisation for fund-raising on behalf of Kenyan wildlife. The Kenyan safari company of Ker & Downey, one of the oldest established safari firms which, until the mid-1970s, existed primarily to provide game for shooting, has also made steps towards the conservation of game, and rhinos in particular. In 1986, the company donated a seven-ton, four-wheel-drive Bedford lorry to the Kenyan Department of Wildlife Conservation and Management, specifically for use in the Rhino Rescue Project. The vehicle has been used to transport captured rhinos from areas in which they are under threat to sanctuaries where they might be safe.

This is all done on the assumption that if tourism is to use the wildlife, then it should contribute towards its upkeep and is not so far removed from the attitude the white hunters had – and have: that is, if the wildlife is destroyed, so is their income. It is a matter of protecting one's environment as well as one's livelihood. In short, it makes sound economic, social and environmental sense.

Hunters still have a large part to play in the conservation of rhinos. Their time may be past in general terms and there will never again be the huge hunting safaris that there were in the first half of the twentieth century. This, I feel, is to the considerable benefit of the rhino as well as all other wildlife and wild habitats.

The sentiments of past white hunters often indicate the true sense of conservation. Blaney Percival once said that 'any animal is infinitely more interesting alive than dead' and, certainly, I have spent far more time with white hunters watching animals than I have accompanying them in order to kill. Most of my early natural history knowledge was passed to me by hunters and not by naturalists.

Consider this, in particular with respect to the rhino:

A sportsman of the finest instincts will doubt his own judgment as to the abundance of the game and, accepting the opinion of the African veteran that absolute extinction threatens many species, especially the rhino, will refrain from shooting to the limit of his licence. Entering Africa in such a spirit . . . can do much to reënforce the efforts of . . . officials along the lines of game preservation. The fact that colonial revenues may be enormously increased if the game reserves are made into national parks to which tourists will be attracted in greater and greater numbers is an argument for conservation that must appeal to the most practical. Meanwhile, unless men become imbued with the true sportsman's or the conservationist's ideas, ruthless slaughter will continue to increase, and the early finish of most of Africa's big game will inevitably follow.

These are not the words of a modern conservationist. They were written[11] by the famous American hunter/photographer, Carl Akeley, in 1928.

— 9 —

THE BOUNTY THIEVES

THOSE who have never come across big game poachers, may have formed a mental picture of them from sensational stories put out by Western media or by various international wildlife protection organisations. Such organisations are seeking donations, some under false pretences, playing upon the sentimentality of the public rather than upon their sensibility and rational thought.

The vision is one of an indigenous native (be he African, South American or Indo-Chinese) with a bloodthirsty leer on his face, a skill for organisation, a network of contacts that would do a drug baron proud and a bank account in the local capital, if not in an unmarked deposit box in Geneva. He carries a sophisticated and technologically advanced rifle and wears a bandoleer of bullets of which he has a seemingly endless supply. He stalks the bush or jungle every day and he nonchalantly traps, blatantly kills, heedlessly maims or viciously brutalises any animal he can get in his traps or his gun sights and turn for a profit.

This picture is as inaccurate as saying that all bank managers wear bowler hats and carry rolled umbrellas.

Certainly there are those, relatively and mercifully few in number, who are supremely well-armed, whose motivation is solely pecuniary, who are comparatively wealthy by Third World standards, and who kill without regard for the human or natural consequences of their actions. But to say that all game poachers are armed to the teeth with sophisticated battlefield weapons is to give a wrong assessment of the situation. For there are poachers and there are poachers. . . .

Game 'poaching' in Africa is a comparatively new crime, having evolved only in the last two centuries. It was invented by and

117

introduced into that continent by white men. To understand the poacher and his poaching, one must look at much more than a greedy native with a powerful rifle.

Before the advent of white men, African natives lived in harmony with their environment which they 'farmed'. They lived off the land, so to speak, growing a few crops, keeping meagre livestock and trapping game for food, leather and clothing. In other words, the humans were an integral part of the natural landscape, reacting and interrelating with it and fitting into the natural scheme of things. They utilised their surroundings and, when human numbers in a certain range reached carrying capacity, they either moved into an unpopulated area or nature took over and reduced their numbers by famine, drought or disease.

When white men arrived, the balance of nature was irrevocably shifted. They started to alter sections of land, putting it to agriculture or settlement, changing the habitat and translocating human populations. When this occurred, the natural environment was reduced for animals and natives alike: both of these inhabitants of the bush lost out. The wild places shrank in size and the animals were constricted in their range. An increase in human population began and, to feed this new wealth of mouths, wild animals from the constricted lands were used as food.

As habitats changed, animals were killed in order to protect crops and as a source of food, and so commercial, 'white' hunting began. This was a wholesale slaughter, as has been shown, but the real damage was not only the increasing numbers of killings through hunting, but also the fact that land came under private ownership.

Ranches were established throughout white–occupied Africa, and the biggest mammals became a potent threat to profits and agricultural stability. Lions and leopards killed and ate livestock, while elephants, hippos and rhinos either decimated, destroyed or devoured crops. The predators were shot out on stock farms, and the others hunted to localised extinction wherever there were arable farms. Rhinos suffered badly.

In Kenya, for example, J.A. Hunter is credited with having shot well in excess of 500 rhinos in his life, almost all of them under licence from the colonial government in crop protection drives. When the pioneering Lord Delamere established his two farms in the Rift Valley, totalling over 57,000 hectares between them, at considerable expense he imported from Britain more than 250 kms of 'gameproof' wire fencing which was to prove useless: antelope leapt over it and rhinos simply bulldozed their way through it. The result was a mass extermination of the local rhino population.

Before white men arrived, Africa was common land. Tribes 'owned' certain areas but there was no personal possession of parcels of land. Everyone was in a position of stewardship, and his future and that of his family and people depended upon his protective use of the environment. Whether or not this was an understood dogma, as it was with (for example) the Red Indians of the USA, or just an in-built instinctive urge depends upon where one looks: some tribes had a religious awareness of the need to protect their surroundings, whilst others, like the animals with which they lived, knew instinctively what to do to preserve the *status quo* and, by default, ensure their survival.

Once ownership of land was established, what lived on that land was similarly owned. Therefore, as with the bleak moors of Scotland or the woodlands of England, wildlife was so longer freely available to all who wished to use it.

In the Middle Ages in England, poaching was rife: landless peasants, hungry for meat and stripped of their right to use the creatures of the woodlands which had previously been theirs to harvest, 'stole' them by poaching. Rabbits, deer, partridge and hares were caught on owned land and the punishment for such a crime was severe in the extreme – even the death sentence. Today, poaching continues in Britain: salmon are taken from Scottish rivers and pheasants from East Anglian farmland. They may not be eaten by their captors, but they are sold as a means of making a living: methods have changed but the principle remains. The pheasants belong to the farmer and the poacher steals them for his own use.

Extrapolate this scenario into Africa and one has the same process going on. 'Peasants' are poaching animals for their own use.

If this type of poaching was to remain the norm, it would not present the same problem for it would be comparatively small scale, the animals killed would be of the more plentiful and more quickly reproducing varieties, such as antelope, and the habitat would be little affected. J.A. Hunter, noted not only for his famed killing of rhinos but also for being one of Kenya's most important early conservationists and an ardent (and very successful) apprehender of game poachers, pointed out that occasional poaching by natives in a hard year did virtually no damage to the natural world. It is

119

prolonged, large-scale commercial poaching, particularly of large species (elephant and rhino) that wreaks untold damage.

The underlying problem is that, although the animals do not theoretically belong to anyone – be they the 10,000-hectare range rancher, the 500-hectare pineapple plantation farmer or the 1-hectare native banana-copse-and-maize smallholder – they actually belong to everyone, and it is the role of everyone to protect them as if they owned them personally.

Game poaching is wrong not only because it is a crime, not only because it causes untold suffering to animals and not only because it is often unjustified (as in the case of the rhino, for example). It is wrong because it is an abhorrent waste, an uncontrolled and unreasoning misuse of a renewable natural resource, and an often unnecessary and reprehensible squandering of nature's considerable bounty.

African poachers fall roughly into three categories and whether they are poaching rhino or dik-dik is neither here nor there in the long run. They are still killing a wild creature without restraint or control: and this is what poaching is, and how it should be regarded.

The first type of poacher is not far removed from the English villager of 500 years ago. He is the subsistence poacher.

The human population of Africa is vast and increasing rapidly: Kenya has the highest birth-rate in the world. Whilst many Africans move into urban areas to seek employment, there are those who remain in the bush living a more or less traditional life subsistence farming, or growing just enough to have a little left over to sell in a local market or at the side of the nearest road. These people are poor. They may choose to be thus, and they most probably treasure their traditional way of life, but they still would like to have a few of the basic amenities of modern life – a school, a church, a clinic. They do not want to own cars, and a bicycle is their most treasured (and useful) possession.

However, because of their poverty, they are reduced to slash-and-burn farming methods. Put simply, they move into an area of scrub bush, hack it down, burn it off and plant it. The soil is often impoverished, the cost of fertilisers prohibitive and the land is not improved. Indeed, these semi-itinerant farmers suck its goodness out with their seasonal crops, leaving it barren before moving on to another location. They may have a few stock animals – a few goats (the most destructive animal ever born) and perhaps a cow, but these cannot be slaughtered: they produce some meat (from kids), milk and in the case of the cow may be a beast for the plough.

In order to obtain meat for their families, these farmers subsistence poach. They enter game reserves or untouched areas of bush and, without licensed permission – and therefore without control – kill game which is made into biltong (sun-dried cured jerky) which they and their neighbours eat or which they sell locally.

I find it hard to criticise these people. After all, they are doing what bush natives have been doing for tens of thousands of years. They are living off the land. The trouble is that the area they can live on can no longer support them and their removal of meat on the hoof causes, less dramatically and more insidiously, as much if not more damage as does their decimation of the cover for temporary agriculture.

The second sort of poacher is what I call the local franchise poacher.

The system works like this: in a town there lives a man who trades in valuable game products – rhino horn, ivory, lions' claws or teeth and so forth. He is known as an 'uncle'. He has capital to invest and he requires a certain amount of merchandise to maintain his business. He is not a poacher but a trader. He offers franchises to natives in the bush to poach on his behalf.

Either the uncle has a gun or two, or he has access to ammunition. His *modus operandi* is to go to a village and find a man who is willing to poach for him. He supplies the firearm and/or ammunition and gives an order for, say, two rhino horns by the next moon. He agrees a set price and the poacher poaches. When he has killed and returns with the merchandise, he is paid, returns the gun (or what is left of the ammunition) and waits for another commission.

Needless to say, the uncle is a powerful man. He is never reported to the authorities; he will wreak terrible vengeance on anyone and their family who informs on him and he is, therefore, generally immune to prosecution. The poacher is invariably the one to get caught.

Once in possession of the merchandise, the uncle sells it into the network, transporting it via one or more middle men to an end user. Quite often, the illegal game products are shipped with other contraband. I know of a shipment of ivory which was smuggled out of Zambia in 1987 with the hollows of the tusks packed with

121

mandrax, an illegal narcotic, and raw emeralds.

The third category of poacher is the highly organised poaching gang.

Throughout Africa, these are most frequently Somalis, sometimes Ethiopians. They come from the Horn of Africa, that part of the continent which has longest been in contact with the Arab world into which much of their merchandise is sold.

The gangs, which can number as many as forty men, are well armed with AK47 assault rifles or the equivalent, move with military precision and are utterly ruthless. If they do not deal in game products, they will deal in slaves. They attack whole villages, pillage and rape and murder at will, steal children for sale as domestic slaves or catamites in the Yemen and Middle East. They will also kill game indiscriminately and turn it into biltong for sale in areas of starvation. They move their loot sometimes in lone trucks, sometimes in caravans of camels. They are, in short, a guerrilla bandit army which is not fighting to overthrow a government but ravaging whatever it can out of the bush to make a profit from it. They are, like the uncles, reprehensible. They are not trying to survive, like the subsistence or franchised poacher, but to make huge profits regardless of the damage.

An indication of what these utterly ruthless men are like can be gathered from the following. In 1990, I spent several days at the Meru National Park in northern Kenya, in the company of Peter Jenkins, the founder of the park. Jenkins, a much respected conservationist and game warden of forty years' experience, knew his park was subsistence poached, but this was not of great concern to him: what he wanted to halt was the wholesale shooting of game and poaching of elephant by highly organised poacher-bandits, known colloquially as *shifta*.

Jenkins' bush telegraph of intelligence gatherers tipped him off that one particularly notorious gang, under the leadership of a man called Gannye, was to enter his immediate area and visit the village of one Yakubdha Ali, a local headman and informer. Gannye, a Somali with a deformed right arm, the result of a bullet wound, who had been operating in the area for over twelve years with a band of eight men, three of whom were armed with automatic weapons, had run roughshod over Yakubdha Ali, demanding food and shelter. Jenkins sent a patrol of nine men out to engage them.

Under the command of Sergeant Adow, the unit silently arrived about 10.30 p.m. at the informer's *manyatta*, a small settlement of a thorn bush *boma* (enclosure) surrounding a low mud hut and out-buildings. From within could be heard the movement of goats and the occasional indistinct mutter of human voices.

The ambush was to be sprung on a path leading from the *manyatta* to a second, smaller *boma* some 300 metres distant. The rangers stealthily deployed into a U formation, the open neck towards the *manyatta* with the path running down the centre.

It was agreed with Yakubdha Ali that, at a pre-arranged time, he would lead Gannye out of the *manyatta*, taking him along the path to the second *boma* where a meal would be cooked and served. To identify himself in the night, Yakubdha Ali would wear his custom-ary white *kanzu*, a long flowing robe. As Gannye entered the U, he would be taken by the rangers at the moment the informer passed through the bottom of the deployment. But Gannye had smelt a rat and, although they could not know it, the rangers and Gannye arrived at the *manyatta* at about the same time, the bandit tipping off his men.

For a while, nothing happened. The appointed time for Yak-ubdha Ali to appear passed and the new moon rose. Then three figures appeared from the *manyatta*. Sgt Adow was perplexed. He had expected two, Yakubdha Ali followed by Gannye. He could not make out who the leading two men were, but he saw, momen-tarily, a glint of moonlight on the barrel of Gannye's gun, slung nonchalantly over his shoulder.

As the three men entered the neck of the U, Gannye stopped and, with the alacrity of a leopard, swung his rifle on to his crippled arm. He fired a short burst sideways, shooting the other two men in the back, killing them instantly. He then sprayed the surrounding bush.

At the same time, Sgt Adow pulled off a long burst, firing low to allow for the rise of the automatic weapon. The other rangers also returned fire both at Gannye and at one of his gang who, having fled the *manyatta* from a different direction, was putting up a desul-tory and ineffective covering fire from some distance away.

The fire-fight lasted less than forty seconds. One ranger was hit in the arm: a bullet passed through the magazine of Sgt Adow's wea-pon and then the palm of his hand, shattering the bones and sever-ing the tendons. The two dead men were the informer's sons. Gannye was killed outright

After this, it was suggested Yakubdha Ali move his *manyatta* nearer to the patrol base. He did this, but a *shifta* hit team of twenty bandits came eight weeks later and gunned him down.

Such is the nature of the organised poaching gangs. Fighting them is not just a matter of protecting animals and habitat but operating as a military unit against insurgents. The prize is not government and power but the safety, beauty, bounty and peace of the natural world.

I have met a number of African poachers – not in the organised gangs like Gannye's but of the subsistence/franchised varieties. They all have several points in common which it is important to know in order to appreciate the underlying motivation and acceptance of poaching.

The first two poachers I met were in the Luangwa Valley of Zambia. They were sitting in the shade of an acacia tree to the trunk of which they were handcuffed. They had been caught ivory poaching and had had in their possession three tusks. Each man was dressed in a tattered T-shirt and shorts: both were barefoot and looked no different from any other African making his way from one village to the next. They did not have a bloodlusty leer and were frankly rather pathetic.

My conversation with them, which took place in August 1987, through an interpreter for I do not speak Chinyanja, went more or less as follows:

What have you been poaching?

Some elephants. One kudu (a very large antelope). Some other things.

Have you been poaching leopards or lions?

No.

Why not?

There is no use for them.

How many elephant did you shoot?

After some hesitation – Four.

But you have only three tusks. You should have eight.

One elephant had only one tusk. Two ran away.

Had you hit them?

Yes.

Those two elephants would, of course, have died a lingering and painful death.

What of rhinos?

A shrug and a small laugh – There are no rhinos here.

124

What would you have done with the ivory?

This question elicited no reply: the two men looked at the ground and avoided my stare.

Would you have sold it to an uncle?

This produced an exchange of looks which I took to be an affirmation.

How much would you have been paid for the ivory?

Another exchange of looks – Fifty *kwacha*. (At that time, this would have been about £5/US$10).

Per tusk?

Per tusk.

And the kudu?

We ate the kudu and we made biltong for our own use. It is not for selling.

They were armed with a modern but much-worn AK47 and a homemade *bunduki*, a sort-of shotgun affair with a crude barrel made out of piping. It was a muzzle-loader.

Who made this *bunduki*?

One of the two admitted to this: the other volunteered a little proudly that he owned the modern rifle.

Where do you get your ammunition?

The 'gunsmith' said he made his but did not say how he obtained the powder: the rifle owner kept quiet about his sources.

How long would you have lived on the *kwacha* you would have been paid?

For a moment, they discussed this before saying that they and their families would have lived 'for a while' on the money. This was not a surprising answer for many bush Africans do not have a concept of extended time. They can think up to a few days ahead but speculating beyond that is not a skill they have acquired. I subsequently found out that the money from the ivory would have maintained the men and their extended families, for the villages thereabouts were many of them occupied by interrelated family clans or groups, for about six weeks.

With the permission of their captor, Clement Mwale, the head ranger for the area in charge of the Anti-Poaching Units (APUs), I gave each of the poachers a cigarette and let them share a beer out of the box in my vehicle. This broke the ice somewhat and I sat on the ground with them rather than squatted on my haunches before them.

What will happen when there are no elephants left? I asked.

There will always be elephants.

But if you shoot them all, what then? What will you do to earn money?

We shall not shoot them all. When these elephants are gone, more elephants will come. From the land over the river. From over the escarpment. This has always happened. It will always happen.

But what if those lands have no elephants?

They both laughed. It was clear to them that this white man was either a fool or someone without a grasp on the realities of the bush.

There are elephants there.

But there were rhinos here until ten years ago. Where are they now? Have more come for those that were shot?

There was a silence for a moment then their reply.

They will come. It is early yet. They will come after the rains.

The truth was that there were about twenty rhinos living in the greater area of the Luangwa Valley, so thin on the ground that these poachers had not yet discovered and killed them. A decade before, the population had been in excess of an estimate of 2000 animals.

These poachers were simple men, bush natives for whom the horizon was limited to a fifteen km radius of their village. They were quite incapable of appreciating the larger situation – which is not surprising: if they could not foresee a future more than a month ahead, when the life-giving and supposedly rhino-giving rains were due, why should they be expected to foretell the doom of an animal which had been present in their locale for thousands of years and was recorded in oral folklore that went back to the dawn of time?

Of course, it is upon this simple ignorance that the uncles play and their business depends.

It is my belief that if one could positively illustrate the damage caused by poaching to these ordinary bush folk, and give them some other way of earning a modicum of income, then a fair degree of the activity would cease, for the ordinary native is still very close to the earth and would wish not to harm it in the long term.

The punishment that would be meted out to the two poachers would have been three months in jail. This was hardly a punishment and more of a holiday: in prison, they would be well fed, have a roof over their heads in the rainy season and would not have to struggle to survive. They might have had to work, but not very hard. The imposition of fines was pointless: they had no money.

126

There was for these two men no incentive to cease poaching whatsoever.

I asked them if they also subsistence poached: both admitted that they did, on a fairly regular basis, but using snares not guns.

These poachers' lives are not only hard but also potentially dangerous. They risk not so much imprisonment as being shot by the game rangers, killed by wild animals or by their own guns. I met one old poacher who no longer followed the profession and who had only one arm: his home-made gun had exploded and blown it off. His brother was less fortunate for his home-made gun blew his head away.

The reason the subsistence or franchise poacher hunts is because it is the only thing he can do to feed his family. There is no other source of employment for him whatsoever. It might be argued that he could farm, but the local economy, such as it is throughout much of Africa, can seldom support such a trade – not to mention the soil which is often very poor.

The only income the local people can get is what they can derive from their environment, which means that poaching for animals is the only available resource. In short, the wildlife is all that can stave off ultimate human starvation.

This predicament, which is rife the length and breadth of sub-Saharan Africa, is played upon by the uncles and those who ultimately buy the produce – ivory, rhino horn, hippo tusks or whatever.

It takes no feat of thought to realise that the person who ultimately pays the poacher to poach is the end user – the Westerner or the wealthy Asian.

And yet, consider this: if we do not buy, then the bush African faces starvation.

This is a dilemma the suggested answer to which will come later in this book. First, though, let us consider the economics of poaching.

An African rhino carries two horns on his nose. The primary, foremost – sometimes called the anterior – horn is the larger of the two; the secondary horn is seldom more than 20–30 cms long. The primary horn is worth about £15–20/US$30–40 to the franchised poacher who pulls the trigger. It is difficult to put an exact price on the item, for this fluctuates greatly: a black rhino horn would have been worth this amount to the two poachers I met handcuffed to the tree. In other words, it would have been worth about three months' living wage. Certainly, this had been the price on offer the year before when there were still a reasonable number of rhinos in the area, being poached by local franchised operators.

As each rhino has two horns, a poacher may make as much as £20–30/US$40–60 per dead rhino, on the assumption the rhino has both its horns which would usually be the case.

However, if the poacher receives £15 or so for his rhino horn, the uncle sells it into the network for £100–175 (US$200–350) depending on the size and quality of the item: in other words, the profit margin is huge and the risk and outlay nominal. The horn then changes hands through middle men until, eventually, it can be worth as much as £25,000/US$50,000.

It is plain to see that the poacher himself is being short-changed in no uncertain way. He gets a bare 0.1–0.15 per cent or so of the potential market value of his commodity. His labour, his skills and his commodity – his wildlife – are being undersold and undervalued.

And this is a seminal point: it is his wildlife. He is the dweller upon the land of the rhino who shares the resources of that land with the rhino and in moral terms the rhino should be his to use and to profit from.

In my opinion, everyone, and especially the rhino as a species, is a loser in the poaching business, except for the few unscrupulous uncles and traders.

The local native poacher is a loser because he is being cheated for his product and labour; the environment is being cheated because it is being ill-managed and abused; the rhino is being cheated because it is dying without any true value being put upon its life, either fiscally, morally or emotionally; we are all being cheated by the fact that the considerable riches of the environment which, ultimately, is the responsibility of every single human being, are being squandered by greed.

The crime lies not in the needless death of the rhino, though this is bad enough, nor the muzzle of the poacher's gun, but in the attitudes that exist which allow such an act to occur.

In other words a rhino's, or any other animal's, death is not a crime if it is justified. The point is that there can today be virtually no justification for the shooting of a rhino throughout most of Africa. Yet the right to use the rhino (or any other animal) does exist and rests with the local native people who may – and should –

A black rhino cow with her calf.

White rhino feeding in a typical rhino habitat of scrub bush.

A black rhino – note the ear listening to the photographer,
the head tilted to attempt a sighting and the head raised to sniff the breeze.

A black rhino browsing – note how the upper lip has turned the twig into the mouth.

A black rhino with passengers – ox-peckers scouring the hide for parasites such as ticks.

Communally-minded white rhino at a small mud wallow; mud wallows are frequent meeting places.

A lonesome black rhino cow and her calf, wallowing.

Black rhino in the Masai Mara of Kenya: two members of the pitifully small – yet largest – remaining black rhino population still living in the wild, and in an unfenced area. This population has yet to reach fifty individuals.

have a moral prerogative to use it should they need to. And, assuredly, the subsistence and franchised poacher does need to utilise the rhino: it is one of the few resources of the bush which can be metamorphosed into hard cash.

This is the crux of the argument: if it is best that the rhino or its fellow bush-dwelling creatures – or the very bush itself in which it lives – not be used, then it is up to us, the rest of the world, to remove the demand for that animal. This has to be done not only by refusing to purchase its products but also by making it worth the while of the local 'owner', whom I prefer to see as a guardian by inheritance rather than a proprietor by right, to conserve it.

It is no use moralising to native poachers about the need to save rhinos and their environment. What must be done is to show them that this conserving is vital to all, including the poacher himself. It is a matter of education and, simultaneously, a matter of filling the economic void the cessation of poaching would create.

Furthermore it must be realised by all concerned that every animal, ultimately, belongs to every single human, because we have the power to destroy it and the responsibility to maintain its security.

This is not to say that we should not use it. After all, in the long run, what is the difference between the cow and the rhino? I suggest there is none. We need cows for leather, dairy products and (for those of us who will not deny our carnivorous ancestry) meat. Thus we have decided to protect it, encourage its survival and use it.

This is what we must do with all wild animals and their habitats. We must save them because we need them. We may need their rain forest to protect our atmosphere, we may need them for their meat or we may wish to protect them because we feel morally obligated so to do. Some we may simply wish to keep for aesthetic reasons, although I disapprove of this.

The reason we should preserve animals is because they have the right to live and because they are a part of the scheme of things into which we too fit. All creatures use each other, either directly (lion eats zebra) or indirectly – consider the myriad of creatures who live on rhino dung middens and their insect inhabitants.

It must also be remembered that man is one of the animals which has a right to live in a certain place. The lesson that has to be taught is, of course, the basic lesson of all conservation. It comes from a Hindu saying based upon animist belief – live and let live. In this

129

phrase is the essence of creation and existence: we must allow all things to live and prosper even though we may use them for our own survival.

Something must be done to stop the scourge of game poaching. Not necessarily to stop the killing of rhinos in the long run, although, at the present time, this must be the case, for the indiscriminate slaughter of the past 150 years has brought the animal to within a horn's length of extinction. There are too few left in the world to condone the loss of even one for any reason whatsoever. And the something which must be done will have to be radical and effective from the start, unlike most rhino protection programmes so far which have failed abysmally.

— 10 —

THE RHINO AND THE AK47

THE AK47 is the standard Soviet military assault rifle, frequently known as a Kalashnikov after its manufacturers, Avtomat Kalashnikova. It is gas-operated, which is to say that it is an automatic weapon capable of firing its entire magazine of 30 bullets in a matter of three seconds. The weapon has a high muzzle velocity: the bullets come out of the barrel at the very high speed of 600 metres per second. The bullets are comparatively small, being just 7.62 mm calibre, more or less the same size as a .22 rifle slug. Not only the Russians make the weapon: variations or copies have also been manufactured in Romania, Bulgaria, Poland, Yugoslavia, Czechoslovakia and mainland China.

It was designed to kill a puny animal, a 75 kg man. It is the rhino poacher's favourite weapon.

Africa has, over the last forty years, been rife with anti-colonial independence wars, and the nationalist fighters have been equipped by foreign powers, often those of Soviet or Communist leaning. It follows, therefore, that Africa is awash with automatic assault rifles of Russian origin or design.

Today, one can buy an AK47-type rifle in Somalia for as little as US$50. For this sum, the purchaser gets not only the rifle but about 200 rounds of ammunition as well. Many of the Ethiopian rebels obtain their guns in Somalia, buying them from Arab gun-runners who bring them in from the Yemen and the Persian Gulf. So, too, do the Sudanese terrorists. And, it follows, so do Africa's game poachers.

The poacher's method of shooting a rhino is cruel in the extreme.

A single small calibre slug, such as the AK47 fires, is not likely to do a great deal of damage to a rhino, which ideally must be killed with a brain shot. This, as any game hunter will be quick to point

131

out, is not easy, even with a far more powerful weapon designed especially for hunting. Sir William Cornwallis Harris discovered the resilience of the rhino when, in 1836 whilst on safari in what is today Cape Province of South Africa, he was obliged to shoot a white rhino to feed his native porters. It took half a dozen 2 oz (56 g) bullets in the rhino's shoulder merely to bring it down.

For a clean and immediate kill with a modern weapon, a rhino must either be shot through the eye, from side-on to the target but a fraction forward of centre, or from behind through the base of the ear. In this manner the hunter achieves a brain shot, the only humane way to kill an animal with a gun.

The poachers, however, lack this skill and a suitable rifle. Few of them have telescopic sights and fewer still care. Not only is the AK47 bullet too small but it is also comparatively soft. Striking a rhino's substantial bone will deform or deflect the bullet, considerably slowing it and reducing its potential for damage.

Furthermore, especially in the case of the black rhino, the poacher seldom sees the whole animal: all he is likely to sight is a part of it in thick cover. That part is often the hindquarters of an animal moving away from the threat.

This actually plays into the poachers' hands. Unable to bring a rhino down cleanly, they fire a whole magazine of bullets into the animal's rump. This consists of a three-second burst of 30 rounds. The idea is not to kill the rhino but to disable it by hitting the rear pelvic joints – the rhino's hip – thus rendering its hind legs useless. In considerable pain, the animal then either runs on with its legs still just operating, to come to a halt in a kilometre or two, or it collapses on the spot, semi-paralysed. If it runs, it can be tracked.

Quite often, however, the rhino gets away mortally wounded. The AK47 'lifts' as it fires: that is, the barrel tries to move skywards under the force of the departing bullets. It takes a well-trained soldier (or poacher) to hold it on its target. Therefore what often happens is that the rhino is sprayed with bullets all around its hind quarters.

On several occasions, I have come upon rhino carcasses in the bush that have 'got away' from the poachers. These animals have been riddled with bullets but remained strong enough to outrun their would-be killers. They have sometimes travelled over ten kms before dropping exhausted to die of their wounds and thirst. Twice

I have seen the scavenged remains of dead black rhinos with their horns still intact.

Poachers do not always follow up wounded animals. First, this may take them nearer to a warden's post: secondly, they may have come upon another animal and killed that more readily: thirdly, they know that a wounded rhino is a very dangerous animal to track.

When the rhino finally drops, the poachers will go to it and usually axe the horn off as if it was the stump of a felled tree. Quite often, this is done whilst the animal is paralysed but still fully conscious. To hear the particular shrill scream a rhino issues as it dies is one of nature's most terrible sounds. (I, fortunately, have never heard it in the wild, but I have had a tape-recording of it played to me: it is the worst, most heart-rending dying sound of any animal I have ever come across.)

In some ways, the rhino which dies in front of an AK47 is lucky compared to those which other poachers target.

Some rhinos are snared. This may surprise the reader: one has to ask what kind of a snare can take a 3000 kg animal with the strength of a military armoured vehicle. The answer is a clever, simple set of snares made out of wire cable a centimetre thick.

The snare consists of two traps, one for the animal's neck and another for a foot. The wire is formed into a noose on a running loop with the ends firmly attached nearby to stout trees. Obviously, these snares are not set up at random in the bush. They must be laid where the rhino is sure to pass – the obvious setting is on one of the regular pathways rhinos use to go to water, the snare usually set close to the water in order to stand the greater chance of being successful.

To kill the odour of the wire and of the presence of men, the poachers either smear the nooses with crushed lantana leaves (which smell strongly of domestic cats) or with fresh elephant dung. They may sometimes be intertwined with the stems of creepers to further camouflage them. The neck noose is hung fairly high off the ground for black rhino, lower for white. The foot noose is supported on sticks at an angle so that the foot enters the noose unimpeded but knocks against the other side of it: the nooses are usually laid to catch animals going to water rather than leaving it.

The rhino walks into the neck noose. As soon as it is snared, it reacts as any animal does in the circumstances. It tries to back away, tugging. The noose tightens. The tighter it gets the deeper it bites and the more enraged and terrified becomes the animal. Eventually, the animal succumbs to the wounds, having first pulverised the bush around trying to get free. Usually the rhino dies from strangulation, or sometimes from loss of blood or the rapid onset of gangrene. The poacher, of course, cannot approach his quarry until it is quite dead.

I have come upon various parts of the skeleton of a rhino which was snared scattered about an area of bush by scavengers: the wire noose had been removed to be set again another day but there were deep score marks in the creature's neck bones. It has been guessed that the animal must have been alive and trying to get free for over forty-eight hours.

On occasion, the wire trace breaks and the animal escapes with the wire embedded in its flesh. If death does not come within a day or two, the animal may spend some months in considerable pain as the wire, which is usually tempered by the poachers by heating, rusts in the wound. The animal may then continue to live, maimed and crippled, with the wound permanently pus-filled and suppurating, attracting flies which lay eggs in it, causing severe maggot infection. It has been known for some rhinos to live in these conditions for up to two years: if they were domestic livestock they would long since have been put down.

Snared escapees are extremely dangerous. There is on record from the early 1960s the case of two fierce rhinos which frequently attacked villagers near the township of Voi, in the Tsavo Game Park of Kenya. David Sheldrick, the famous warden of Tsavo East in which the animals were marauding, was sent to kill them. Upon shooting the animals he discovered that one had been snared by the foot whilst the other had been caught by a wire noose which went around its horn and under the point of its prehensile upper lip. Both had probably fallen foul of light wire snares set for antelope rather than rhinos: at that time, rhino poaching was not so rife as it was to become a decade or so later.

Snaring is, of course, used when firearms are unavailable or ammunition is scarce. It is also used when the use of a firearm might give the poacher away.

This method of poaching is also used on elephant with more frequent breakings free and subsequent torture for the animal. I have also seen an elephant with a badly deformed trunk, the result of it having become entangled in a small animal snare line. The animal was in poor condition and was plainly unable to feed itself properly: it was stripping bark from a tree with its tusks which it then tried to bite off the bole of the tree without the use of its trunk.

Another method of capture, far less frequently used in modern-times due to the availability of firearms and its unreliability, is that of pit-digging.

This technique – or a variation on it, driving animals over a cliff – was used by primitive man and must be the oldest form of trap. Quite simply, a large hole is dug in a likely place, lined with sharpened stakes and covered over with branches and earth to disguise it. The animal blunders on to the covering, falls through, is impaled and slowly dies.

Another time-honoured method of poaching is with a bow and arrow; spearing rhinos is not common because of the need to get close to the prey in order to throw the spear. As black rhino also live in thick cover, the vegetation further impedes the flight of a spear.

The designs of African bows and arrows vary from place to place: those I have seen in Zambia are very different from those shown to me in Kenya, for example, and individual methods of construction are seldom published. However, there is one accurate account of the manufacture of poachers' bows and arrows recorded by Dennis Holman in his book[1] about elephant poachers in Kenya.

The Liangulu tribe, who have hunted elephant for generations, are typical of many hunters of large mammals. Certainly, their hunting equipment is more than adequate enough to bring down rhino which they have also poached in the last twenty years.

The bow appears roughly similar in construction to a traditional English long bow and is usually shaped out of one of five species of wood (two of them of the genus Grewia), the bow-string made from the leg sinews of a giraffe which are twined to give strength. The power of a bow is measured by how many pounds it takes to pull the bow-string back to the extent of the archer's reach. A traditional mediaeval English long bow has a pull of about 70 lbs: a poacher's bow pulls at least 100, often as much as 130 lbs. (As an experienced archer, I attempted to pull an African hunter's bow in 1990: I could not manage to draw it more than three-quarters of its full distance and that was a considerable feat!)

The shafts of the arrows are made from one of four different

135

woods, two of them Grewia but not the same species as those used for the bow.

The arrow is fashioned in three parts: the main shaft, the foreshaft and the arrowhead. The arrowheads are made of iron, often beaten from nails or nowadays cut from steel sheet. They have no standard shape but most arrows I have seen are either of the thin, willow-leaf variety or of the 'Apache' shape, being pointed with two large, razor-sharp, opposed barbs. These are bound to a foreshaft about 15 cms long with a thin twine of gut. When not being prepared for use, they are stored separate from the main shaft, in a protective wallet or wrapping of soft leather.

The foreshaft and arrowhead are fitted to the main shaft by thin strips of gut applied when wet so that, as they dry, they contract. The join is strong but made deliberately so that, after striking the target animal, the main shaft either breaks free or is knocked free by the quarry: this prevents the arrow coming out of the wound. The fletchings (flights) of the arrows are made from the wing feathers of large birds such as vultures and large raptors: I have seen both three- and four-fletched arrows. The feathers are glued into notches on the arrow and secured with twine or woven animal hair.

The main shaft is usually about 60 cms long, the foreshaft adding another 25–30 cms to make a total overall length of 80–90 cms according to the individual owner's reach.

When the weapon is drawn, the whole of the foreshaft projects forward from the bow, the join between the two shafts acting as a stop to prevent the foreshaft from touching the poacher's hand.

The arrow itself has little impact upon the target rhino. It penetrates the skin and lodges in the subcutaneous tissue: in itself it is incapable of inflicting more than a slight wound.

The reason why it is so effective is the same reason for the hunter keeping the foreshafts in a protective wallet and not letting his hands come into contact with them when shooting. These arrows carry a highly lethal poison for which there is no known antidote. The mere touch of this substance on the skin is sufficient to kill. As little as four grams on an arrow will kill a rhino.

Known in Somali and Swahili as *ouabaine*, the poison used is commonly derived from the acokanthera tree[2], otherwise known as the scrub-olive tree. It grows throughout eastern Africa, from Eritrea down to the Transvaal. It has dark green, stiff leaves which look like those of the English laurel but not as shining. The flowers are small and scented somewhat like lilac whilst the fruit are about the size of a grape and deep purple when ripe.

The process of obtaining the poison varies from tribe to tribe but it always involves the prolonged boiling of chopped stems, leaves and fruit and the reduction of the liquid base to a sticky, gum-like consistency. It can be stored for a considerable length of time but will deteriorate in sunlight, hence it usually being kept in small clay pots.

The poison must be introduced into the blood system through a wound: in man this may occur by osmosis through sweat-damp skin. I did not realise this aspect of its potency until I was in the park headquarters of Tsavo National Park at Voi in 1990. In the poached ivory store there, I was studying the sorry stock of recently collected tusks when I saw on a shelf the paraphernalia of a poacher who had been shot in an exchange of fire a few weeks before. His clothes were tattered by bullets and his water bottle, made out of a plastic drinks container, was similarly punctured. His bow hung from a nail and a buckskin quiver of arrows lay beside his clothing. I went to pick up the arrows to look at them when the head ranger, Stephen Gichangi, grabbed my arm. One touch of the poison would have done for me and within a few minutes.

When used in poaching, it is frequently mixed with another poison derived from a comparatively rare African plant, *Sapium madagascarensis*, which when touched causes severe inflammation of the skin. This makes the acokanthera poison reach the bloodstream more quickly. Another ingredient is sometimes a third poison brewed from a small flower, Dioscorea. Some arrow poisons are also laced with the venom of puff-adders or scorpions which act as an anticoagulant, preventing the arrow wound from healing and increasing the ease of flow of the blood in vessels around it. (There is much superstition also involved in the brewing of the poison: for example, to make the quarry run in a straight line when hit, and thus be easier to track, a decomposed elephant shrew is added to the boiling pot.)

The acokanthera poison acts upon the heart in much the same way as digitalis, paralysing it. In a man, this may occur within sixty seconds. In a rhino it takes a little longer. The rhino might run for a hundred metres or so before collapsing. It may not then die immediately but will twitch and thrash in agony for some hours before succumbing. A few may survive, very sick, for up to a day or two but they will assuredly die in the long run.

The favourite place to hit rhino is, as with elephant, in the belly where the skin is less thick and there are no bones to hinder the entry of the arrowhead. Furthermore, the arrow may chance to strike the liver or spleen, helping the poison to disseminate all the more quickly.

Game poaching – including the taking of rhino – with bow and arrow is still widely carried on in East and Central Africa. As with snares, the bow and arrow makes no sound and is of great advantage where silence is important to the escape or lack of detection of the poachers.

For those poachers who have neither bow and arrow nor AK47, home-made guns offer a solution. These are shoddy and downright dangerous Heath Robinson affairs, often considerably more hazardous to the poacher than to the rhino.

I have handled two of these contraptions: one of them had a jagged hole in the 'breech' where it had exploded backwards and removed its owner's face.

They were both crude in the extreme with barrels made out of heavy duty iron piping with a makeshift hammer at the end attached to a strong bar spring. The striker or firing pin was fashioned from a shortened nail. The stock – carved from the hard wood of a mopani tree – was well made: the manufacturers knew how to work with natural substances but the technology was beyond them. (Home-made guns killed many Mau-Mau terrorists in Kenya in the years of their uprising in the first half of the 1950s: it seemed to be the case that if a gun looked like a gun then it would work like one.)

The firing of these guns is as crude as their manufacture. There were no rear sights on the examples I saw, but they had a foresight in much the same manner as one might find on the front end of an English farmer's 12-bore shotgun. To hit even the side of an elephant the hunter must be very close indeed.

The weapons are loaded down the muzzle with a powder charge whilst a detonator cap or somesuch is inserted below the hammer. A wad of cloth or leaves holds the charge in place. The projectile may be a ball-bearing, a round stone or a spent bullet retrieved undamaged from a previously shot carcass. If these are not available, other ammunition is used. Although I have never seen the remains of a rhino shot with one of these guns, I have seen a dead elephant which had been hit some time before by one of these muzzle-loaders. Embedded in its skin were several wood screws, some sharpened bits of iron (possibly nails) and a bottle top.

These weapons are, of course, incapable of bringing down a rhino. They can only cause it pain and, if it is unfortunate, wound it sufficiently to bring on secondary disease or putrefaction which will kill it.

The horrors of poaching and the misery it causes to game wardens and conservationists is poignantly summed up[3] by F.W. Woodley, at the time the assistant game warden of Tsavo in Kenya. 'This park', he wrote, 'is far from being a sanctuary for wildlife. . . . Today we found a terror trail of diarrhoea from a herd of about forty elephant. One had been shot with a poisoned arrow and we came across it after two hours. It was still alive but in terrible agony, and I ended its suffering with a bullet in the brain. This poison is horrible stuff, and the whole dirty business of poaching must be stopped'.

Those words were written on 23 September 1948. In many respects, nothing much has changed since. In others, matters are totally altered but not necessarily for the better as far as the rhino is concerned.

— 11 —

HOW TO CATCH A RHINO

T HE methods employed by men to kill rhinos are fairly simple. Techniques for catching rhinos and keeping them alive and well are somewhat trickier.

In Roman times, the animal was hunted and captured to provide a show in the arena. Rhinos fighting other creatures – including men – were not uncommon in these bloody spectacles and, needless to say, they did not survive long in the amphitheatre. How the Romans captured their rhinos is unknown: I know of no depiction of such a hunt in carvings. After the demise of Roman games, the occasional rhino was caught as a curiosity for Chinese emperors, but rhinos were not really captured in any numbers until the early nineteenth century.

The opening up of Africa from the seventeenth century onwards made Europeans curious. Myths and legends about the 'dark continent' abounded. It was a terrible, disease–ridden, fascinating place of fabulous and fantastic creatures, cannibals and naked black houris, dense forest where the vines were living creatures that twined out at one in passing. The rhino, with its 'armour-plating', its size, its apparent propensity to attack and its unicorn horns was the epitome of the miraculous wildlife. Whilst it was beyond the scope of explorers, hunters and early naturalists to bring home a real gryphon or phoenix, they could produce a rhino.

The very wealthy across Europe sought to obtain such animals for private menageries but soon the trade grew as zoological gardens came into being, as naturalists turned more to being scientists rather than curators of living museums. In those days, rhinos were transported in atrocious conditions and, not surprisingly, a good many did not survive the journey from Africa.

When captured, the animals were hog-tied and transported by

wagon to the nearest seaport, this part of the journey in itself being no mean ordeal. Once on board ship they were confined to crates which gave them virtually no free movement whatsoever. They were fed and watered adequately, although sometimes with inappropriate vegetation, but they could not lie down and were often given added support from poles running from side to side under their bodies. These chafed and rubbed the flesh sore: the skin on the belly of a rhino is remarkably soft. Those to survive the journey were often in poor condition on arrival.

In more recent times, rhinos have been captured for safari parks, in the course of translocation and for use in films.

It is interesting, as an aside, to consider the image of the African rhino in the movies: it is usually that of an awesome and dangerous animal which threatens the lives of the main characters. In the 1950 production of Rider Haggard's famous African story, *King Solomon's Mines*,[1] a black rhino acted its part well and was as seemingly ferocious as the screenplay demanded. That the animal was a semi-tame rhino raised by human hand goes without saying.

In 1952, the rhino took a less pleasant role in the filming of Ernest Hemingway's story, *The Snows of Kilimanjaro*.[2] Based loosely upon Hemingway's shooting safari experiences, the rhino was going to have to die and the production was given a one-rhino licence. This was before the modern American cruelty and protection laws that govern film-making with animals were passed: such a script requirement is today illegal and has given rise to the industry of making life-size, lifelike automaton wild animals.

In due course, a black rhino was hunted and shot both on film and with a bullet. However, when the rushes (unedited film) were viewed by the director Henry King, he was appalled. The killing of the rhino looked on film to be nothing more than a cold-blooded gunning down and so the whole sequence was edited to look as though the animal had died in a noble and dignified manner.

The rhino has not always suffered in filming. Susanne Hart, a wildlife veterinary surgeon who became well-known in the 1960s for her television series *Animal Ark*, recalls a rhino which was being used in a feature film being shot in Kenya. In order to keep the rhino docile on location, it was doped (which would also be disallowed by today's laws), but this did not work effectively. The rhino became obstreperous in front of the cameras and temperamental in its holding pen. Eventually, after some time during which the rhino

141

spent its waiting hours charging and head-butting the timber walls of the pen, it broke its primary horn off. As the main characteristics of a ferocious filmic rhino were its sharper attributes, this placed the film crew on the horns of a dilemma. At last, it was decided to fit a rubber horn which, when glued in place, looked as good as the original. The film was shot and the rhino looked as ferocious as was intended. Only once did it falter when, hoisting a tree-trunk, the horn bent much to the surprise of the owner.

It is sad that rhinos have always played villains: this is certainly not type-casting. Other, far more dangerous species have been filmed for both the cinema or television including lions, but the friendly animal films have been restricted to actor dolphins, kangaroos and chimpanzees. These are supposedly cuddly: dolphins are benign but kangaroos can have a nasty temper and both bite and punch dangerously. Anyone who has seen chimpanzees hunting other monkeys in the wild – and they themselves harbour cannibalistic tendencies – and has been the subject of a chimp attack will appreciate that man's nearest animal cousin is not necessarily his friend. Perhaps it is time for a feature film about the life of a rhino: as calves they are as cute and as frisky as lambs, as bumblingly charming and gangly-legged as a new-dropped fawn, yet they grow into one of the most magnificent animals on earth.

Even advertising has taken on the tough image of the rhino. A British telephone network advertisement in the 1980s used a rhino charging (more blundering) into an office and the Japanese car makers, Suzuki, have a rhino depicted on the rear of their four-wheel-drive town jeeps.

The earliest method of catching a rhino was to round it up on horseback and drive it towards a trap of some sort. The traps were usually a funnel of bushes set in with heavy stakes hammered into the ground.

This method was not always successful because, by the human activity of building the funnel, the local rhinos were alerted and kept away, shifting their territories. Furthermore, halfway down the funnel, the rhino would begin to realise it was being manipulated so it would veer off to one side and ram through the funnel sides. Only the strongest construction was effective.

At the neck of the funnel either a stout timber pen was constructed or a series of strong rope nets hung to entangle the rhino, both being camouflaged with branches. If the rhino did not breach the pen and did ensnare itself in the netting all was well: however, the animal not infrequently went straight on through the pen or disappeared into the bush with the net rope trailing from its head.

Other methods of capture included driving the rhino into a gently sloping and narrowing pit constructed rather like a Second World War tank trap. The idea was that, once down in the pit, the rhino would be unable to reverse out and would, therefore, be easily tethered. Another technique was to drive the rhino over a series of trip ropes tied between trees then, once it was down, throw netting over it. Yet another procedure was an extension of the poacher's snare, a series of ankle nooses into which the rhino would step of its own accord whilst making for water along a communal path.

All these methods were, to a degree, successful but they also all involved potential and often serious injury to the rhino. What had to be devised was a means of capture without harm.

This was eventually perfected by the white hunter turned animal trapper and trainer, Tom Carr-Hartley. The Carr-Hartley family were extraordinary, larger-than-life folk for whom the bush was an entire way of life. Tom Carr-Hartley owned a game farm near Thomson's Falls in Kenya: one of his sons was the child star who played Jungle Boy, a sort of child Tarzan, in an early television series in the 1950s; his wife was mauled and killed by one of their pet 'tame' lions.

Once, in about 1958, I visited the Carr-Hartleys' farm. It was then a centre for holding animals en route to zoos and safari parks with some animals kept for filming roles and the like. I recall there was a black rhino in a pen to which I fed twigs through the slats in the timbers: its foamy saliva on my hands was hot and sweet, the air pushing out of its nostrils was humid and rumbling as if blowing from a deep volcanic cavern. There was also a baby rhino not more than a few months old, which juddered its nose into the backs of my knees, and a number of big cats – mostly lions – in cages. The highlight of the visit, I remember, was being able to stroke, pat and even hug a cheetah, the only time I have ever had such a rare and privileged opportunity.

Carr-Hartley hand-reared rhinos as well as other game with a care and expertise that was and remains rare. His capture technique was as careful.

The problem with catching a rhino is that it is so huge and is in motion as it is caught. Brought down, it falls heavily. Carr-Hartley devised the means of lassooing rhino from an open, moving chase truck.

Although I never saw this done, I understand the hunt went like this: a rhino was spotted and, after a time of stand-off confrontation and maybe a charge or two, the animal would realise that it was up against a winner – perhaps the lorry became a sort-of mechanical dominant bull – and would decide to retreat. Once on the run, the lorry chased after it with (I seem to remember) Carr-Hartley sitting on the front in a metal chair affair welded to the bumper and bonnet. He was armed with a long pole from which dangled a rope noose. Drawing alongside the rhino, he would slip the noose over its neck and the lorry would then start to slow down gradually. So would the rhino. In the end, both would come to a standstill and the rhino would be secured by being gradually winched to the lorry and his feet tied.

The idea of lassooing game was not new. Carr-Hartley had himself used this means of capture on giraffe, no doubt having known that this was how Charles Cottar had caught the same creature in the 1920s, the result being comparatively humane, but rounding up and capturing rhino with a vehicle was probably first carried out by Carr-Hartley. Since then, rhino round-ups with vehicle and (especially in South Africa) helicopters are commonplace.

Today, rhinos are infrequently apprehended for zoos and safari parks. These places now have established breeding herds and can supply each other.

If a rhino is caught nowadays, it is in order to radio-tag it (by affixing a small transmitter to the animal, often suturing it in place on the thick hide, so that it might be tracked and studied from an aircraft or with a satellite), to study it scientifically, to dehorn it or to translocate it.

This latter aspect of conservation is at the centre of big game management, control and husbandry. Translocation is an extreme method of conserving the species, but it has to be accepted, for the rhino's situation is extreme and drastic measures are now called for.

The concept of rhino translocation is surprisingly not new. It was first mooted in 1930 when an American naturalist, Dr Herbert Lang, who had visited the Umfolozi game reserve in 1925, and was seriously worried about the fragile chances of survival of the white rhino, suggested that some be captured and reintroduced into areas where they had previously been known.

144

Basically, translocation is just what it seems – the moving of a rhino from a habitat where it is under threat to one where it is secure. The threat may come from habitat destruction, poaching or a need to thin out a population without culling.

The first substantial translocation programme was established in the early 1960s by Ian Player, brother of Gary Player, the famous golfer. The aim of the project was to move white rhinos from threatened areas into safer habitats. He worked primarily in the Umfolozi game reserve in what is today KwaZulu, the Zulu homeland in South Africa.

The scheme was so successful that Player subsequently had sufficient animals to sell overseas: some of his white rhinos are still alive today and have been breeding successfully in captivity.

I came across four of Player's translocatees in Longleat Safari Park, in the south of England – two bulls and two cows – and I saw another one elsewhere. Originally six were sold to Longleat but two have since been transferred to other places, one of them being amongst the first white rhinos to be shipped to Australia.

I have driven alongside the Longleat rhinos, both in a saloon car and on the keepers' tractor, and have stood in the rhino house next to the biggest of the bulls, Panzer, who is about 1.85 m. high to the top of his hump. He is a glorious animal, at times cantankerous but at others mild and amenable. I have scratched him behind his ears and under his foreleg which he raised to encourage me, and I have had him jam his horn against my thigh as if to remind me of his power and what he could do if we had met in the wild.

Most of those translocated to other African countries have, however, long since been poached. I know of the deaths of six sent to the Meru National Park in Kenya, killed at the hands of *shifta* bandits. Of the four sent to the Livingstone Game Park near Victoria Falls in Zambia, none survive: the fate of the last to die, the fifth of Player's animals I came across, is shown in the photograph facing page 65.

'Operation Rhino' in the late 1960s and early 1970s, the translocation programme operated by Ron Thomson in collaboration with others, transferred many black rhinos from the range of poachers.

A large number of animals had to be moved and this demanded an efficient, safe and fairly quick method. What was developed by Thomson from the earlier methods used by Player, and has since become the staple method for almost all big game capture, was darting.

145

The concept of darting was invented in the USA in the early 1950s when deer were brought down using small air-gun darts mounted with small engineering drill bits coated with drugged honey. It was a crude system but it worked. Then, in 1957, the first special dart was made.

The darting of rhino requires a special skill, an expert knowledge of rhino physiology and behaviour and a very cool nerve indeed.

The dart is fired from a special sort of rifle called a capture gun (sometimes spelt Kapchur). Before the gun became widely available, or because some game rangers distrusted it in the early days, cross-bows were sometimes used instead. The original capture gun was invented by a man named Red Palmer who, with a team at the University of Georgia in the USA, developed an 'anaesthetic gun' using compressed carbon dioxide from a soda siphon cartridge as a propellant, rather than an explosive charge. These first weapons, known as Palmer capture guns, were not very reliable and it was Ron Thomson who, amongst others, refined them towards being the far more effective weapon that they are today.

The modern capture gun is smooth-bored, like a shotgun, with a very large calibre barrel. It is a single-shot weapon: that is, it has no magazine and must be reloaded for each shot. When fired, nowadays more commonly using an explosive blank charge, it goes off with a very loud report and it has a powerful recoil. It fires not a projectile but a dart.

The dart itself is a cross between a very large bullet and a hypodermic syringe. It varies in size but those used on rhinos are about the same size as a Havana cigar tube. At the rear end there is a bung of cloth which holds the dart in place in the rifle barrel and acts much as a wad does in a muzzle-loader. At the front end is a very strong hypodermic needle about 8 cms long. Inside the tube of the dart is a chamber into which a drug is put in front of a plunger.

There are variations in this design but the basic principle is the same. Some earlier darts used different methods, including acid to eat away at release mechanisms: in some, the plungers moved too easily and the drugs were lost. All the early darts had to be carried needle upwards which was dangerous to those carrying them and made stalking awkward: rhino-stalking takes all one's attention and to think of the needle was an unwelcome distraction.

The dart leaves the gun comparatively slowly. One can follow its progress through the air with the naked eye: a poacher's arrow travels much faster. When the dart hits the rhino, the needle pene-trates its hide. The sudden loss of forward movement gives the plunger momentum and it is forced into the front of the dart thus injecting the drug into the target.

As with the idea of translocation, the drugging of rhino was not a new idea, even in the 1960s: the first rhino to be felled with drugs was a black rhino shot in 1927 by an American hunter called Harris. He used an ordinary bullet smeared with a curare derivative.

The drugs used have been developed over the last thirty years. Originally, they were provided specifically for downing large wild animals but they are now widely used in general domestic veterin-ary work, in safari parks and zoos as well as in the wild.

Early drugs caused problems – Flaxedil[3] caused respiratory problems, Largactil[4] could cause a loss of blood pressure and prevent the drugged rhino from regulating its body temperature while Hyoscine dilated the pupils of the rhino's eyes. Other drugs were unreliable because it was difficult assessing the correct dosage for individual animals. Some (like Sernyl) were effective with black rhinos, calming them down, but aggravated white rhinos into hyperactivity.

Today, the rhino is darted usually with a cocktail of two drugs, M99 and Fentanyl.

M99, otherwise known as Immobilon,[5] appears as a yellow liquid and comes from a family of drugs known as etorphines which are a form of opiate having been developed from morphine. It is very potent in tiny doses.

M99/Immobilon is a reversible neuroleptanalgesic drug which sends the recipient to sleep with no pain. In large animals it may be administered either intravenously or intramuscularly: it is, there-fore, ideal for use in rhino darts for it does not matter where the animal is hit, so long as the drug goes in well under the skin.

This drug, however, has a dangerous side effect. Before depress-ing the nervous system and knocking the rhino out, it produces a period of stimulation during which the animal is hyperactive and, in the bush, may well damage itself. It might also 'damage' those trying to capture it. It is for this reason that the dart contains another drug.

Fentanyl, to give the drug its trade name, is a rapid anaesthetic over a thousand times more potent than the commonly used pethi-dine. It can be long-lasting and, because it is fast-acting, it prevents the excitement caused by the M99.

Just as with the poachers' acokanthera-based poison, the drugs can be of great danger to man. One milligram is all that is needed of M99 to drop an adult rhino: a mere used needle scratch, spillage on to human skin through which it may be absorbed, or splashing on to the eyes or lips, require immediate rectification. Luckily, unlike the poisoned arrows, there is an effective antidote known as M50/50 or Revivon[6]. The rules of handling M99 or Immobilon decree that there must always be a second person present to administer the antidote by injection, should this be necessary.

The M99/Fentanyl mixture works fairly quickly. It does not pole-axe the rhino but takes up to twenty minutes to knock it totally unconscious. The dose must be assessed fairly accurately: Ron Thomson has told me of several rhinos he has darted, followed until they dropped and approached ready to set to work upon them only to have them stagger to their feet and groggily make a go for him.

Once the rhino is down, the darting team must set to work quickly. The drug concoction will not keep the rhino sedated for long and there is always the danger of individual side-effects. The technique used these days is to get the rhino down using M99/Fentanyl, then quickly inject it with a third drug, azaperone, giving this intramuscularly and at a good depth. This done, the M99 antidote is given.

Azaperone is a commercially prepared tranquilliser often used on domestic pigs to prevent excitement, aggression and fighting when litters are put together for the first time on a pig-rearing farm. It is also used, not always to good effect, to tranquillise rhinos whilst they are being transported during translocation. However, given in substantial doses, it will keep a rhino sedated for up to eight hours. The drug is particularly suitable for such large animals as rhinos because although it induces a very deep sedation, it does not significantly reduce cardiac output or heart rate. It also prevents any depression of respiration which might occur with other drugs.

The darting of wild rhinos is a hazardous occupation. I know of several game wardens who have assured me that except for facing well-armed poachers, it is the most dangerous part of their job.

The darting is done by a team of men. This ideally consists of a tracker, the darter, his assistant, a porter-cum-tracker, and a moving crew of men who approach only once the rhino is sedated.

A darting hunt can never follow a set plan. Rhinos are not predictable. Generally the tracker will find the rhino which it is intended to dart and will note its territory.

The hunt begins at first light with the animal being tracked: it is best not to have the rhino unconscious during the hottest part of the day, so that it won't overheat or get heat-stroke. Once the animal is located, the darter begins to stalk it in the company of his assistant who is armed with an ordinary rifle. If the darter looks like being seriously attacked and killed, the assistant will have to kill the rhino. Fortunately, this is a very rare occurrence.

The capture gun does not have a great range nor is it anything like as accurate as an ordinary firearm. The darter must, therefore, get as close as possible to the rhino before firing. Not only this: he must also have a totally uninterrupted shot, for the dart, being slow and cumbersome, can be deflected by something even as insignificant as a grass stem.

All the while, the porter must not be far away. He has the antidote, medical equipment for both human and rhino first-aid and the azaperone syringes.

The rhino first-aid kit is important. If the rhino is not finally brought down before the day gets hot, it must be protected. The drugs – particularly azaperone – can quickly dry out the mucous membrane of a rhino's eyes, thus blinding it permanently, so damp cloths have to be put over the side of the head and drops of streptopen are periodically put into the eyes. The animal must be kept generally cool and must not be allowed to dehydrate. To this end, saline drips are sometimes carried.

As the darter gets close to the rhino, within fifteen metres, the atmosphere is tense. The rhino might run or charge. Everyone is on tenterhooks. When the darter fires, the rhino starts to run. Ideally, the dart is fired into the rump. In this way it hits solid muscle, sticks well in to the hide and will not be so readily rubbed off if the animal instantly charges into cover.

It is not uncommon, however, for the dart to miss or deflect off the rhino. If this happens, it may well be time to climb the nearest tree.

If the rhino is hit, it must be followed at all speed. This can mean a sprint through thorn bushes, over dried up *dongas*, through razor-sharp grass tussocks and over rocky or sandy terrain for up to a kilometre or two.

As soon as the rhino is found, assuming it is lying on its side in

149

more or less open ground, the antidote and azaperone have to be given, the eyes covered and the mouth and head rested upon a cushion of leaves. This is to prevent it breathing in dust and dirt whilst unconscious. If possible, the rhino must be assisted with breathing by not placing undue pressure upon its ribcage. When lying on its side or being rolled over unconscious, there is a risk that a lung may become deflated by the pressure of the other organs upon it. Indeed, it is best that the creature be positioned upright, lying on its tummy so to speak, to avoid internal organs pressing against each other and causing longer term damage.

Whilst the rhino is unconscious, the opportunity is always taken to measure it, take blood and other samples and perhaps give it antibiotics to treat the wounds on its sides. Long-lasting antibiotics[7] are given. Cortisones are never administered as they may cause females to abort. Streptopen is used not only on the eyes but also on the open wounds and any wounding caused by the dart. In some areas, rhinos may also be marked for further identification. This is done by ear-nicking. If a drugged rhino is to be dehorned, the base of the horn is treated with antiseptic powder in case of infection and to kill off any fly larvæ.

What follows is the difficult part. The rhino must be moved.

In South Africa, where the infrastructure of bush roads in game parks and reserves is well maintained, the darting teams always try to drop their quarry close to some sort of vehicular access, rounding it up with vehicle or helicopter to a convenient location. In the early days of darting and translocation, the rhino had to be picked up often from far into the bush, and this required cutting and forcing a track for many kilometres.

Once sedated, the rhino must then be manhandled by the moving crew on to a lorry. This is no mean feat, for a bull rhino takes considerable shifting. Ropes are used to get the rhino on to a flat bed of planks rather like a sled, which is then hauled by hand on to the rear of the lorry. All the while, the animal must be monitored and protected from injury.

Moving a 3500 kg rhino is harder than recovering a crashed vehicle. It has no wheels: cranes cannot be used. The rhino is moved entirely by brute - but careful – force.

Once on the lorry, the rhino is usually taken to a very strong timber-lined pen where it is allowed to recover from the drugs. As the rhino regains consciousness it becomes belligerent and is very dangerous. For some hours after coming round it is confused and will attack the pen walls with such force that it may break off its primary horn. However, the rhino quickly calms down after becoming fully conscious. The black rhino 'tames' more quickly than the white but does not become quite so docile when in long-term captivity.

After some weeks, the rhino is tranquillised and put into a trans-portation crate for its road journey to its new and safer location. In order to acclimatise the rhino to the crate, it is attached to the animal's holding pen and is used as the feeding area. The rhino is not unconscious during the period of loading and transportation and is coaxed to walk on to the transport vehicle rather than be hauled on by ropes or pushed from behind. This in itself is a difficult task for the rhino is intelligent enough to know not to get on to the lorry and it can only be cajoled aboard if it is dopey.

Once at its destination, the rhino is again kept in a holding pen for some days in order to acclimatise it to its new habitat. It is then released. The holding pen may well be erected in the rhino's new territory, placed in an area where it will not come into immediate conflict with previously translocated animals or other wild rhinos already established in the locale.

Darters and darting teams have had many narrow escapes. Stories are legion, some of them humorous, some of them frightening, some of them downright thrilling.

Imagine, if you can, a rhino being darted and then disappearing at top speed into heavy cover. It takes over an hour to track it down but, at last, it is seen ahead under an overhang of branches, well in the shade and lying propped up against the tree trunk snoring blissfully. The sun has kept off it, which is good, and it will not have been placed in any jeopardy for having finally dropped in such a spot. Take hold of the medical bag and walk towards the rhino, ready to give it the azaperone and M50/50 shot only to find it suddenly on its feet, wide awake and setting off on a charge from a distance of twenty-five metres. In dense rhino populations, this is a not uncommon error that might be made: the doped rhino is else-where – this is one that was taking a nap.

Darting team members have been badly gored by rhino, severely injured (even after the animal has been put in the holding pen) and permanently maimed and even killed. Ron Thomson was once hit by a rhino which then attempted to trample him. He had the

151

presence of mind to keep himself under the animal's belly, allowing himself to be kicked to and fro between fore- and hind legs like a football. So long as he remained under the animal's belly, it would not be able to crush him with its head, stamp on him or gore him. He was not badly injured, suffering only a large number of grazes and severe bruises, escaping eventually by rolling out from under the animal as it made off into the bush.

The loss of rhinos today through translocation is minuscule. The Natal Park Board in South Africa, for example, has a death rate of less than one per cent: of the approximately 1000 rhinos translocated in the Umfolozi/Hluhluwe reserve only five have died and of these four were sickly when captured.

Rhino translocation has been very successful. It was the first system by which large, wild animals were moved long distances and rehabilitated elsewhere. Without translocation, and the bravery and determination of people like Thomson, the rhino's survival plight might well be even more drastic now than it is.

— 12 —

GOLDEN HORNS
AND OTHER RHINO PARTS

WITH rhinos having been poached near to extinction, why has this animal attained such importance and financial worth?

It would seem as if the rhino should be valueless save perhaps as a source of meat, yet even that is frowned upon in some societies. Many South African tribes would eat the meat of the white rhino which was often shot by early explorers as food for their porters. On his 1844–51 expeditions and safaris in South Africa and Bechuanaland, William Cotton Oswell fed his porters in this way, on one occasion shooting six rhinos with six consecutive bullets within a distance of a kilometre: such was the density of some rhino populations then. Many East and Central African tribes, however, would not consume the flesh of the black rhino because it was thought to pass on leprosy. This belief still exists widely today.

Rhinos were also frequently considered to be the animal homes of evil spirits, and to kill one would be to let these spectres free. Many tribes consider that there is no effective exorcism for the spirits passed on by the rhino, and the hunter who first throws his spear at a rhino or strikes it with his first arrow is regarded as a hero, for his action will assuredly have drawn him to the spirits' attention and he will soon die. Unfortunately, this piece of superstition does not seem to have been passed on to those who indiscriminately poach rhinos.

With such superstition relating to the rhino it is hardly surprising to discover that Africans have little use for it. The only native utilisation of rhinos that I know of is with the Masai who used to carve clubs out of rhino horn on the assumption that they endowed the owner, when fighting with his club, with the enormous power of the animal.

153

Europeans have been known to eat rhino. Many Boer hunters, who shot rhinos for a variety of reasons (one of them being to make *sjamboks*, rhino-hide whips), considered the hump of a white rhino to be a delicacy. It was cut off at the spine, like a fillet, and baked in clay. The tongue of the black rhino was considered another delicacy – Burchell was very fond of it boiled like ox tongue – and early settlers in Kenya, the Rhodesias and Natal made rhino-tail soup. David Livingstone, the explorer and missionary, also ate rhino on his various journeys, and was sufficiently far-sighted to say that the white rhino would soon be exterminated: his reasoning, however, was somewhat awry as he suggested it would disappear because of the culinary quality of its flesh.

Unlike the leopard, zebra or giraffe, the rhino does not have an attractive skin suitable for tailoring fur coats; its hide can make leather but the cost of this is generally prohibitive because of the complexities of processing; unlike the elephant, it does not carry two hefty chunks of ivory projecting from its face. The rhino really has only its horn and this has been its downfall.

Once Africa started to trade in earnest with Europe, and wild animal products began to become fashionable, it was inevitable that uses would be found for the rhino's horn. True horn, such as that of stag or ox, has long been used decoratively as knife handles and, to a lesser extent, as jewellery, but with the advent of rhino horn yet another unusual commodity arrived in the market. The vogue reached its height in the second half of the nineteenth century when it almost for a time overtook ivory as a commodity, particularly when elephants started to get shot out of easily accessible country in southern Africa. Traders were quick to exploit this market and by the 1880s it was in full flood. European and native hunters worked tirelessly to supply dealers and one Arab trader went so far as to arm 400 Matabele warriors with firearms specifically in order to shoot rhinos.

A wide range of personal items were made from rhino horn: I have seen cutlery and manicure sets with rhino horn handles, snuff boxes carved out of blocks of horn, brass document seals mounted on horn and even rhino horn combs for holding hair in place, inlaid with silver, gold or ivory. These items are today very scarce on the antique market and consequently valuable.

This trade put paid to the white rhino south of the Zambezi river. The extent of the harm done was noted by Selous who, in 1879,

154

hunted for eight months in Bechuanaland without seeing a sign of a single animal. Visiting a European trader there, he wrote, 'His store always had huge piles of rhino horn, the spoils of a hundred animals at one time. They were sold to traders and eventually made their way to England.'

Another use for a rhino, and one I find particularly distasteful – on a par with the old practice of making waste-paper bins, coffee tables and umbrella stands from elephants' feet – was that considered by George Eastman. He undertook an extensive six-month safari in Kenya in 1926 and wrote of his reasons for shooting a rhino:

> 'This morning we went out again, and I got a topi (for meat for the men), a rhino which I killed with the double barreled 470, another impalla and an eland that is close to the record (30¼ inches). The rhino's horns are nowhere near as good as Audley's, but I was afraid I might not have a chance at another, and I wanted the skin for my new library table top.'

In time the fashion for rhino horn in Europe passed, just as all fashions do but, in one part of the modern world, the horn of the rhino remains not only fashionable but socially important. That place is North Yemen, and particularly the capital city, Sanaa.

When a young Yemeni boy reaches the verge of manhood between the ages of twelve and fifteen, he is circumcised and, as a symbol of this and his entry into manhood he is presented with a *djambia*.

This is a ceremonial dagger which not only confirms his mature status but is also a symbol of the dedication of his life to the Mohammedan faith. Yet the *djambia* is more than just a personal adornment, for it is central to many traditional dances in which it is brandished over the dancer's head and it is used in tribal courts when litigants symbolically hand their daggers to their sheik as an indication of their trust in him and his honour. From time to time, the *djambia* is used as a weapon of retribution in feuds but, by and large, it has only a ceremonial significance.

It is worn tucked into the belt and is contained in an intricately wrought leather scabbard, the decoration of which declares a man's tribal roots and his position in his society. The substance from which the handle is made also denotes rank, status and wealth and those who are of high position have even more artistically made weapons. The most impressive, inlaid with gold and silver tooling, are those of the Sayeed families who are said to be the direct descendants of the Prophet Muhammad.

In the past, the handles of *djambias* have been made from a variety of horns including those of cattle, many antelope, zebu, rhino, ibex and giraffe, the latter being very fashionable in the 1940s and 1950s.

However, with the enormous increase of oil revenues in the Persian Gulf and other Arabian peninsula countries in the late 1960s, and especially after the boom of the oil crisis of the early 1970s, many Arab men could afford even more elaborate and expensive *djambias*. Those made from rhino horn, often considered historically to be the most prestigious, were suddenly much sought after, and the trade in horn, which had existed for hundreds of years, increased dramatically to meet the new demand.

In past centuries, the rhino horn trade had been conducted only with African countries under close or frequent Arab domination such as those in the Horn of Africa (Somalia, Ethiopia, coastal Kenya) or lying near to the Sahara over which Arab land trade routes ran (Sudan, Chad). Some horns were obtained by slave traders moving deep into Central Africa (Zambia, Zimbabwe, Zaïre) but by and large the trade was geographically restricted.

With the sudden explosion in demand for rhino horn, all of sub-Saharan Africa came into the sphere of trade and vast quantities of horn were imported into Yemen by way of Sudan and, to a lesser extent, Somalia. In just eight years from 1969, it is conservatively estimated that over 23,000 kgs of rhino horn passed through Sudan. To supply this, nearly 10,000 rhinos gave their lives and about 20,000 *djambia* handles were carved. Between 1970 and 1986, the world population of black rhino crashed from an estimated 70,000 to just over 4,000: 65,000 rhinos died to meet the dictates of Arab fashion and the other major uses of rhino horn.

For not all of the horns of these unfortunate animals ended up decorating fancy daggers. Some had a far more lucrative and – to western eyes, perhaps – bizarre destination.

For over two and a half thousand years, the rhino's horn has been imbued with magical properties. How this came about in the first place is conjecture.

Contrary to a universally held Western misconception, the rhino's horn is not widely considered to be an aphrodisiac. Only the Romans (and, nowadays, a few Indians) believed it to have this property, presumably either because it is long, hard and pointed upwards or because the rhino itself is so generously endowed by the size of its penis and takes over an hour to complete its copulation. This is the only time that rhino's horn has been given a medicinal value in Europe, although its value merely as a wondrous object associated with the unicorn existed for hundreds of years. In some countries in the Old World, however, it was considered an ill omen and best left alone: a horn in the house was said to be unlucky in many parts of central Europe.

In the Far East, however, it is another story and rhino horn has been on the books of traditional herbalists and exponents of folk-medicine since well before the time of Christ.

Traditional Oriental medicine has long espoused the beneficial attributes of animal products. The eating of tiger's flesh brings on courage, the possession of the neck bones of a tiger protects the owner from tiger attack, the rubbing of tiger's fat on to the limbs both protects and cures against arthritis and rheumatism. Whilst the eating of flesh and collecting of bones is merely superstition, there is a well-found reason for rubbing the fat on the body. Just as long-distance swimmers coat themselves in grease to retain body heat and exclude the effects of water on the skin, so might fat act in a similar way. To a sufferer of rheumatism, the warmth and exclusion of dampness would relieve their symptoms somewhat. There is a good deal of simple logic behind the less audacious claims of many folk-cures: my grandmother kept a small jar of goose fat in her medicine cupboard to rub on chests and prevent colds.

There may be some truthfulness in the effectiveness of goose fat but some of the claims laid against rhino horn are, to say the least, far-fetched and verging upon the miraculous.

A good deal of the veracity of Oriental medicine depends not so much upon chemical effects of individual brews of potions – such as aspirin might have upon blood vessels - but upon the philosophical, religious and psychological abilities of the various so-called drugs, knowledge of which is based upon centuries of study.

Much of Oriental medicine is scientifically verifiable and those who rub Tiger Balm (made of various herbs, fats and opiates, none of them derived from tigers) upon their aching muscles or sip ginseng tea to enliven or invigorate themselves are not wasting their time. Even the consumption of snake's blood, said to clean and revitalise the system and cure anæmia, is not ridiculous: snake's blood is rich in iron. Much of the basis of the traditional medicines is superstition but just as much is based upon truth. Not only this, but faith in the product plays an important part in the prescription of Oriental medicine much as it did in European medicine in the Middle Ages and still does in African tribal medicine. (I have heard of a man dying from the bite of a non-poisonous snake: he died because he believed he would. Conversely, I know of an African who was 'cured' of fits by a rancid concoction of butter and herbs administered with a modicum of chanting.)

In this faith, and not in some miracle chemical manufactured by rhinos, lies the power of their horn.

Depending upon where one looks in the Far East, rhino horn has a variety of wonderful properties[1]. In India, it is still – though very infrequently – offered as an aphrodisiac when mixed with herbs and swallowed in milk or honey: it was from the East that the Romans heard of this supposed property. Similarly taken, it is also said to cure arthritis, muscular pains and spasms and paralysis: fat and stomach lining are also said to cure polio and skin diseases. In the past, the horn was burnt under the anus of hæmorrhoid sufferers to alleviate their condition and to counteract constipation.

Not only the horn is considered efficacious. Strips of woven rhino hide are worn as rings and anklets to ward off devils and were also regarded as an additional cure for hæmorrhoids. Rhino's fat, dung and urine is believed to cure skin ailments and the urine, when drunk, is considered to have aphrodisiac qualities and be good for throat infections. Dung mixed with eucalyptus oil is prescribed for muscular pains.

These claims are largely bogus although there may be some basis to the horn being a cure for constipation, for it might provide roughage if taken in large quantities: certainly, singeing the rear end of piles sufferers with burning horn will do them no good. The urine is only thought to be an aphrodisiac because it comes from one of the biggest penises in the animal world and as for the dung curing aches and pains, it is clear that it is the eucalyptus oil which does that job.

Not surprisingly, the parts of India which have longest had a trading link with Africa are those in which rhino medicine is most common – the ports of Bombay and Goa have for centuries been the main trading posts for rhino products.

Elsewhere in the Orient, it is the Chinese who place the most medicinal value upon the rhino.

The belief that the rhino has magical curative powers has been well established there for over two millennia: that the creature itself was highly prized as being a mythical beast – a sort of unicorn – has already been shown.

It has been the horn of the Asian rhinoceroses which has been considered the most effective as a medicine but, with the decline of the Asian rhinos in the last two centuries, the Chinese have turned to the African rhinos for their supplies, dosages being increased because the African rhinos do not apparently have the concentrations of power of the Asian ones.

The use of rhino horn is fairly extensive and most Chinese traditional medicine shops in Hong Kong, Singapore and throughout Malaysia and China hold a good stock of horns. Indeed, wherever there is a resident expatriate Chinese community, rhino horn may be obtained, even in London and even where such provision is illicit.

Prescriptions vary according to the individual practitioner but most involve shavings of the horn being boiled in a little water or rice wine, sometimes with added herbs or animal products, then drunk by the patient.

I have – just once in Hong Kong, to satisfy my curiosity – tried a cup of rhino tea, for want of a better word: mine was just shavings with no added ingredients simmered in half a cup of water. The flavour was weak, barely discernible and reminded me vaguely of the taste of chewed fingernails such as I knew it as a nervous child.

Rhino horn shavings are given as a treatment for the lowering of fever such as typhus and malaria. The idea, as is so often the case with such traditional brews, is that the liquid cleanses the body of poisons. Additionally, it is regarded as a cure for laryngitis, bronchitis, tuberculosis and poor eyesight. As in India, the hide is used for skin disorders. Dried and powdered rhino's blood is sold as a tonic for sufferers of anæmia which it probably does help to cure being, like snake's blood, rich in iron. The truth, however, is that almost any blood will help and in some parts of Asia 'artificial rhino's blood' is on sale, probably derived from cows. The urine is used to cure chills and chest infections.

In the last two decades, the rhino has suffered from Oriental medicine sellers as it has at the hands of the *djambia* makers. With

159

the increase in wealth in the Pacific Rim economy countries in Asia, promulgated by the industrial and technological advances of Japan, Hong Kong, Taiwan and South Korea, there have come into being those with the money to afford expensive exotic medicines.

Luckily, due to the very technological advances that brought these nations their wealth, Western medicine has also increased in popularity and availability and this has reduced the reliance upon some forms of traditionalist cures. Nevertheless, many Oriental universities offer courses in both Western pharmacology and traditional practices.

That Oriental medicine does offer a viable alternative to Western medicine is undeniable: ginseng is a very good general tonic and blood (for example) can combat other circulatory deficiencies. It would be wrong to dismiss such Oriental skills as massage and acupuncture and herbal remedies tried and tested over thousands of years. However, what must be overcome is the mumbo-jumbo rather than the specific curative qualities of such 'natural' medical teachings.

As a result, rhino products and rhino horn in particular have become very valuable. Claims that rhino horn is worth more than its weight in gold are far-fetched, but it has become sufficiently valuable as to make the risks of poaching and trading worth taking.

We have already seen that a single horn is worth several months' income to a bush African. To the end user, or the last middle man in the chain, it is worth far more.

As a *djambia* handle, the horn is worth somewhat less than it is to a medicine dealer: a good quality dagger can sell for up to £10,000/US$20,000. In Hong Kong, however, a traditional medicine dealer will pay up to £35,000/US$70,000 for a large primary horn, possibly much more. As has been mentioned, the poacher receives less than 1 per cent of this sum which, although he may be pleased with this amount, is still a travesty which leaves him – unwittingly – cheated.

Sadly, this does not necessarily bother him. The following is another part of the conversation I had with the two handcuffed poachers.

Do you know how much a rhino horn will sell for in China?

They shrugged: China, I realised then, is an incomprehensible place to them, just as it would be to a five-year-old child. I rephrased my question.

How much do you think the uncle sells the horn for to the man who wants to buy it?

They sipped at the bottle of beer and muttered briefly to each other.

One thousand *kwacha*. (At that time, about £100/US$200).

No, I replied, he will sell it for 250,000 *kwacha*.

This figure was beyond their grasp: it was like explaining the first prize in a state lottery or the football pools to a beggar. They made no response. I tried to explain that this was sufficient money to let them and their whole little village live without working for more than the rest of their lives.

At this, they both laughed uproariously. I remembered that the distant future was, for them, too vast to be contemplated. When they stopped laughing one of them spoke.

We are content, he said.

This state of affairs is criminal. What I feel should become of that money I will mention later: suffice to say now that 250,000 *kwacha* would have paid for the entire running of the anti-poaching units throughout the South Luangwa Valley for two years, increasing manpower by 100 per cent equipping all the rangers with modern new guns, walkie-talkies and several Toyota jeeps. And that's just the death of *one* black rhino.

The answer to the rhino horn trade and the eventual forced cessation of it is a complex matter and requires many different approaches. It is not just a matter of banning trade as has been done with ivory. Some of these approaches are working efficiently, some are not: some are bizarre, some outrageous and some most definitely ill-advised.

In the field of traditional Oriental medicine, there are successful moves being made to persuade practitioners that rhino horn is no more efficacious than other animal horn products.

Ersatz rhino horn is now coming on to the market and substitutes are being advocated – one such is the horn of the saiga, an antelope which is farmed commercially in Russia, the horns being a by-product of butchery which would otherwise be burned or reduced to bone meal. If a patient has faith in the product, then that is usually sufficient for it to work and it is gradually happening in a few areas that traditional medicine dealers and doctors are persuading their clients that other horn is just as good, if taken in slightly larger, but not necessarily more expensive, doses. This tactic is having some effect, but it is slow and requires the re-education of traditionalists and the education of a new generation of pharmacists.

Whatever rhino horn is used for, there is a ready, eager market for it and this will continue until the rhino is utterly extinct and supplies of horn expended.

Or there might be another scenario . . .

Let me pose a supposition. Let us assume that the bush was still full of rhinos and that we could turn the clock back, say, twenty-five years. Let us also assume that, at that time, it had been agreed to make a legal market of rhino products and build up a trade in rhinos just as if they were cows. Under those circumstances, what could the rhino be used for?

First, its horn would be of value, a luxury market already established for it (*djambia* handles) and a very lucrative traditional medicine market in Chinese communities around the world.

Secondly, despite its production cost (which, ironically, might well increase its attraction), the hide could be made into luxury leather goods on a par with eel-skin, high-grade pig- and calf-skin or ostrich leather. (I do not know what rhino leather looks like, having never seen George Eastman's library table, but I have seen hippo and elephant leather goods and they are as good as – and often superior in quality to – ordinary cow leather.)

Thirdly, its meat could be marketed where supersition does not forbid its consumption. There has long been a value placed upon exotic meats throughout the world and rhino steaks would fit into that niche.

Again, as with rhino leather, I have never eaten rhino but I have on just one occasion eaten elephant. It was very tasty and like many game meats very low in fat.

At this point, let me give an aside which shocked and horrified me the first time the fact dawned on me. I was in the bush in Zambia going after poachers and came upon a dead elephant which had been shot: it was the one riddled with odds and sods of trash and a bottle top. The animal had died for its tusks and was left rotting in the bush. Over two tons of prime protein, superb meat wasted when only twenty kms away I saw little African children with their bellies distended for lack of protein. This, to me, is the evil of poaching, of bad or ineffective game management and of a collapse of global game and environmental policies. If that elephant had been butchered it would have relieved a lot of local suffering and quite possibly have reduced the need of the local people to poach. After all, they went for ivory to turn into money to buy food.

Fourthly, the bones of the rhino could be ground down and sold not as fertiliser (although that might be a possibility) but as medicine to the same people as would buy the horn. The toe-nails could go to the same end user as would the testicles and penis of bull rhinos.

The offal could be used as fertiliser but would probably prove to be uneconomic. The teeth could make curios for those who wish to buy such bizarre trinkets.

In short, most of the rhino save its intestinal tract and gut would have a guaranteed commercial value.

Even whilst the animal was alive it might earn money as some in captivity do today. A number of zoos in the Orient which hold captive rhinos do collect the dung and urine for sale to traditional medicine dealers. This begs the thought as to whether or not Western zoos, strapped for cash, realise how much potential income they hose out of their cages and enclosures each day.

Let us suppose that we could legally sell a dead rhino on the open market. It would be worth, at a random guess, over US$60,000, perhaps more. It would satisfy a demand, it would realise its true price, it would not be wasted and its death would not have been in vain: quite the opposite, in fact, if the conditions below can be made to apply.

I agree that not much of it would be of real use to mankind: no one will cure their bronchial illnesses, piles, lower their fever, tone up their blood or improve their standing with the ladies. But if they are prepared to pay, why not let them buy? If a fashionable lady wants a rhino-skin handbag, let her have it.

Yet there are and must be conditions – that the rhino lives naturally in its wild habitat, it dies humanely, trade in its parts is regulated and the money goes back to the rhino's local environment – both human and animal – to protect, conserve and enhance it.

And, of course, that the rhino is not an endangered species.

Would it not, I suggest, be wonderful if we had so many rhinos back on earth that their future could be so secure that they might be used in a scientifically controlled way, with legal selling and no abuse?

So much for dreams.

None of this is possible now because the opportunity was lost through ignorance and lack of foresight: the greedy men have had their day and are, at the expense of the rhino and the rest of world, working hard towards an imminent end to both their avarice and the rhino itself.

— 13 —

ELECTRIC FENCES, PERSONAL ALARMS AND RHINOS

THE rhino has been at the forefront of wildlife conservation for nearly twenty years. Along with the other big mammals – elephants and whales – it has captured the attention and the hearts of the public and with justification. It is an astonishing and wonderful animal.

Many different concepts have been applied to its protection, some of them general to all other forms of wildlife as well, others specific to the rhino.

The animal poses a number of unique and difficult conservation problems which must be appreciated.

A rhino is large and can be killed in a comparatively easily manner, simply because it provides a substantial target: a poacher has to be particularly inept if he can't hit it with either a firearm or a poisoned arrow. The product (horn) is conversely fairly small and can easily be smuggled. Rhinos live in well defined, reasonably confined territories and their social routine (visiting water or middens) makes them predictable and therefore (again) easy targets. Existing in very small groups or singly, the rhino is less easily kept tabs on by game rangers and, again, this works to the poachers' advantage for it means that there is not a herd instinct which can provide advanced warning of approaching danger. The black rhino also requires a particular habitat in which to live.

Conservation of rhinos is, therefore, split into a number of differing criteria all of which must be met. Saving the rhino is not just a matter of sticking up a notice around a suitable environment, declaring it a game reserve and employing a few rangers. It requires a concerted and very well co-ordinated plan of action.

So what is being done at present to save the rhino?

The most obvious effort is that of organising effective game

165

departments, most of which have existed for decades, having been started during the years of the colonial ownership of Africa. The role of game departments has changed little since their instigation: they were established to control the issuing of hunting licences, to combat or at least contain game poaching, to protect crops and livestock from depredation by wild animals and to protect all wild living creatures from the persecution of mankind. This set of aims remains true today although there is less call now for crop or livestock protection and the issuance of hunting licences, and more for anti-poaching activities and the control and development of tourism.

Also under the auspices of game departments comes the maintenance or establishment of game parks and reserves in which all the wildlife – including rhinos – is protected.

In all game parks throughout Africa, there are warden or ranger patrols. Their roles and responsibilities are various: game control is the most obvious but they are also heavily involved in tourist guiding and control, infrastructure provision for tourism, habitat maintenance, road and access repair and building, habitat protection (from domestic livestock infiltration, for example), public relations with surrounding native populations and, if allowed, hunting control.

In addition to all these tasks, they have to oppose poaching.

Anti-poaching units work in a number of ways depending upon the threat and how it must be tackled.

 In Zambia, for example, the anti-poaching units (APUs) patrol through the bush in small platoons of up to six men. Four are rangers and two general porters who carry the food and establish and guard the bivouac camps. They stay out in the bush on foot for up to a few weeks at a time, living rough, tracking the poachers, hunting them down and, hopefully, capturing them. They not infrequently exchange fire with poachers which can be exceedingly dangerous. The poachers have AK47-type automatics and the rangers are armed with ex-British Army .303 Lee-Enfield rifles which saw service during the Second World War.

The rules of engagement are quite interesting. The rangers draw the poachers' gunfire upon themselves deliberately: they may not – by law – fire until fired upon. However, there is more than a legal nicety to the strategem. The poachers fire and soon expend their ammunition: the rangers then move in with the

166

bolt-action rifles and make an arrest.

APUs are, however, exceptionally ineffective. It is impossible to patrol an area of tens of thousands of hectares of rugged terrain and virgin bush with several dozen men, some of whom must be stood down on leave at any one time and others involved in the alternative multifarious tasks of rangership. It is the equivalent of asking 200 policemen to combat street crime, homicide, narcotics, traffic and race relations in New York City.

Vehicles are next to useless in the bush. They are noisy and give themselves away, they move too slowly, they are costly to run in fuel terms and they break down: also, imported spare parts in Africa are prohibitively expensive. In Kenya, the Anglo-American wildlife charity Friends of Conservation have provided some patrols with camels. These move fast, are comparatively silent, are tall and give a view over the bush, require no fuel and do not break down. They require 'servicing' (by a vet rather than a mechanic) every quarter but that is all. Camel patrols prove effective against poachers not merely because they afford the APUs mobility but they wrong-foot the poachers who are forever on the alert and therefore placed on the defensive.

In Zimbabwe, where Zambian as well as Somali poachers cross the Zambezi river and have hit hard at rhino populations, the authorities regard the game protection situation as undeclared war. There is a shoot-to-kill policy against poachers which does work as a deterrent but not so effectively as might be hoped. Once again, the attitude is to apply military expertise and concepts to combat the poaching. It might be a guerrilla war.

To this end, Zimbabwe rangers are as well-armed as the national army and are a potent fighting organisation. The poachers, needless to say, are also consequently well organised. Further north, in East Africa, Kenyan rangers are many of them equipped with the latest G3 automatics – these are lightweight NATO military weapons which are very powerful, with an extraordinarily rapid fire rate and more than a match for an AK47. They are easy to maintain, have no wooden parts (the stocks being made of carbon composite) and are very reliable indeed.

Ideal anti-poaching weapons are helicopters but these are beyond the finances of all but the very wealthiest of governments or game departments.

One African country – I was asked not to advertise the fact – uses a few old US military helicopter gunships in their anti-poaching drives. Their technique is not to send out noisy patrols of vehicles but individual rangers who live quietly and secretively in the bush. They are armed for self-defence but they are under orders not to engage poachers. Instead, they find them and radio in the location. The gunships then fly in and strafe the poachers. This is proving very effective not only in killing poachers but as a deterrent to others.

Yet this is the exception. For most, the APUs have sometimes shoddy and often inadequate supplies and insubstantial financing.

It may be argued that game reserves have a detrimental effect in that, by concentrating game and wildlife, they make it that much easier for the poacher to find and kill target animals. Sadly, this is a necessary evil of the state of affairs in which we find ourselves today.

However, be that as it may, game reserves also provide an invaluable focus for conservation attention and this can be very successful. Building upon the established infrastructure of a reserve can bring about positive rewards in projects aimed at specific target animals and the rhino is one of these which can benefit quite considerably.

An example of this is to be found in the Masai Mara National Park in Kenya.

In 1971, 108 black rhinos lived inside the reserve. By 1982, after a decade of considerable poaching activity, the population was reduced to eleven animals scattered sparsely over the area. Without good wildlife husbandry, they were not a viable breeding population.

Now, due to the extensive attention of the international Friends of Conservation charity (formerly called the Friends of the Masai Mara), there are twenty-four black rhinos in the Mara, making up the largest breeding population in an unfenced area in the whole of East Africa. Careful management and unobtrusive (but very efficient) protective measures linked to specific fund-raising moves (such as an adopt-a-rhino scheme, and raising money for a vehicle or a bridge over a river) and financial provision have seen the birth of sixteen youngsters in ten years. This attention to conserving and encouraging a specific viable population gives definite hope for the black rhino's survival.

Some methods of conservation are aimed specifically at the horn trade.

To combat the uncles and middle men, some countries – and they are understandably reluctant to admit to this publicly and I respect their secrecy - are manufacturing fake rhino horn out of resin, or an amalgam of resin and cow-horn. I have been shown a number of counterfeit horns alongside real ones taken from either dead rhinos or poachers. Even to the trained eye, it is difficult to tell them apart. Less accurate counterfeits still fool some of the traders, who do not realise they have been duped, until there is a comeback from the end user in the Far East or Sanaa. By that time, the money has changed hands and the dealer has lost his credibility and, in one instance, I have been told, his life. After all, big money is involved.

Another method that has been tried in the wild is to de-horn rhinos, just as a farmer might dehorn his cattle. This causes the rhino no pain – as it might a cow – for the rhino's horn is not supplied with nerves or a blood supply, and is sawn off above the base, so there is no risk of infection, bleeding or living tissue damage. The rhino has merely to be drugged for ten minutes while the sawing is done.

The poacher, it is hoped, will see that the animal has no horn, and will therefore not bother to waste his scarce supply of ammunition on it.

Unfortunately this seldom works with the black rhino which lives in thickets and is seldom seen in its entirety. I have only ever seen a 'complete' black rhino on less than a dozen occasions in the wild. Normally, all that I have spied has been a bit of flank, a bit of rump, or a flicking ear through the dense cover. And this is what most poachers see. They do not wait to ascertain if the animal has a horn or not: they shoot, follow up and arrive at the dead or dying rhino. By then, it's too late. If the rhino has no horn, he died for absolutely no reason – not even a *djambia* handle. And the de-horning will have been in vain.

De-horning white rhinos has proved to be more effective, because the animal lives more in the open, and poachers can see that it is devoid of its value. However, I know of several instances where de-horned white rhinos have still been killed out of spite or to teach the authorities a lesson, so to speak.

Furthermore, the rhino's horn is much more than an adornment to its face. It is a badge of rank, a fighting weapon, a stand-off flag, a branch hook and a salt- and water-digging tool. Take away a bull rhino's horn and you take away his masculinity, his status in his

169

community, his defensive weapon (should he need it) and perhaps even his self-esteem. The only way de-horning would do no harm is if all the rhinos in an area were all dealt with: but that is well-nigh impossible on financial, man-power and practical grounds. And there is no guarantee that it would put an end to the killing.

Diplomacy is being used in fighting the horn trade, too. Lobbying governments and government agencies to combat poaching is an important aspect of conservation, and is being tackled in a similar way to international narcotics and terrorism. Not surprisingly – for poaching rhinos (and other animals) is also a form of terrorism, aimed not at political ideologies, but at the environment which it is far more valuable and worthwhile to save.

Moves to combat the *djambia* market were made in 1986 and reported in *BBC Wildlife Magazine*:[1]

[The ministers of the North Yemen were warned] that if North Yemen – which, through the medium of three or four large traders, imports the horn to make dagger handles – did not try harder to enforce its 1982 law prohibiting these imports, foreign aid, especially from the US, might be reduced. [They were] also reminded . . . of the continuing criticism of North Yemen in the world's press.

Accordingly, a six-point strategy was worked out:

1 The prime minister would talk to the principal trader, who has been buying about two thirds of all imports, and warn him to stop handling new supplies.

2 The foreign minister would discuss with a senior official of the United Arab Emirates [through the free trade ports of which the horn was being shipped] the need to close down the entrepôts for rhino horn in its sheikhdoms.

3 The government would prohibit all rhino horn exports. [Chinese, Koreans and Yemenis were buying the shavings to export to the Far East.]

4 The government would ask the grand mufti to issue a religious edict stating that to cause the extinction of an animal species is against the will of God.

5 When reapplying for their licences, owners of dagger-making workshops would have to agree not to use any more rhino horn. If, later, rhino horn was found on their premises, the shops would be closed.

6 The customs department would encourage water-buffalo horn as a rhino-horn substitute by eliminating import duties on it.

It was an appropriate time to act. The North Yemen government was starting to take action against smugglers on general economic grounds, and to tag on an environmental issue was shrewd thinking on the part of the international conservationist, Dr Esmond Bradley Martin, a long-time rhino campaigner.

The effect was that the North Yemen did implement the entire strategy with considerable effect but it has not entirely eradicated the *djambia* trade. Another force, that of short supply, is killing the sordid business off.

This is, I believe, the kind of direction in which such action to combat the end user in the rhino market should move: it is to explain the situation diplomatically but at the same time to flex political muscle. A possible paucity of foreign aid speaks louder than environmental threat and dogma.

Another conservation alternative is game ranching. Here a private ranch is established which is still a wild place but highly managed with watering pools supplied by bore-holes, fencing to exclude domestic cattle and a localised work-force to maintain the place. These ranches are not philanthropic organisations but profit-making businesses.

Their income derives from several sources. First, it provides photographic amenities for tourists and/or scientists, wildlife filmmakers or naturalists. As these are exclusive and the presence of game is guaranteed, the ranch can justify high charges.

Secondly, the ranch can provide strictly controlled hunting. This is in no way similar to the atrocious game ranching which can be found, for example, in some parts of the USA, where more or less captive animals (lions, leopards, tigers, elephants and so on, surplus stock from circuses, zoos and private menageries) are shot vicariously and very cruelly, sometimes while they are tethered or contained in a small pen or cage. This is abhorrent in the extreme, nothing more than primitive blood letting, and unacceptable in a civilised society.

True game-ranch hunting is close to the real thing. A hunter books in to shoot a certain species of animal known to be on offer, which he then has to track, draw close to and kill. He is on foot (no

171

vehicle shooting is allowed) and there is the element of danger and the old-time safari about the hunt. He is allowed to kill only a certain individual.

Game ranches are a bit like farms and, indeed, some prefer to call themselves farms and exclude hunting. Instead, the whole fauna of the ranch is managed as if it was some sort of exotic domestic stock, shot under controlled conditions to maintain a viable and active breeding population, within the carrying capacity of the land, and bearing in mind the well-being of the indigenous species and habitat.

This seems a sensible approach to me. In some cases, however, there is a drawback where the rancher shoots out major predators in order to guard against too much loss of revenue from meat sales. I believe the predators should be allowed to take their share and be controlled in numbers, not annihilated.

An extension of this ranching concept is the sanctuary. This is best illustrated by the example of Anna Merz's Ngare Sergoi rhino sactuary in Kenya, a 4000-hectare private reserve to the north of Mount Kenya and established upon rolling thorn bush country, an ideal black rhino habitat.

Anna Merz is to rhinos what George Adamson was to lions and Jane Goodall and Hugo van Lawick are to chimpanzees. She is justifiably besotted by them and, in 1976, appalled by rhino poaching and the horn-trade, she and her husband set up the sanctuary. It is not exclusive to rhinos, and also contains resident populations of cheetah (itself endangered like the rhino from human habitat encroachment and the fact that it is at the end of its evolutionary branch), leopard, buffalo, zebra and reticulated giraffe. In addition there is, of course, a wealth of smaller bush fauna. Although originally set up for the black rhino, a small group of white rhinos has been brought in. Both species are breeding.

The concept does protect the rhino but at a very hefty cost. Originally wealthy people, the Merzs have spent all their money on the sanctuary which costs upwards of US$10,000 to run per month. The whole area is surrounded by a 2.5m.-high game-proof electric fence with an alarm system on it to alert the staff to intruders. A small private army of seventy armed guards mount 24-hour patrols.

This dedication is laudable, and Anna Merz, by living in such close association with wild rhinos, is conducting some vital research which is uncovering new information about the two species. How-

172

ever, this cannot be the answer. Such a sanctuary is little more than a vast private zoo and, despite – perhaps because of – the militaristic air of the place, it is a besieged rhino camp with a concentrated population begging to be poached. When the organised Somali poachers do get in, and I feel sure that this is only a matter of time, knowing the dogged persistence of these ruthless *shiftas*, they will act like foxes in a chicken house.

Such a sanctuary can be little more than a holding exercise – a well-intentioned but vulnerable stop-gap – and it has its place in the scheme of conservation. I cannot but deeply admire these efforts, but they must not be regarded as a conservation solution and certainly not as an end in themselves.

Using ranches and sanctuaries to breed wild rhinos is a positive move towards conserving the species. Rhinos are also bred in captivity in zoos and, somewhat more frequently, in safari parks. That these animals increase the global population is excellent but then there comes a problem. When a safari park or sanctuary reaches its maximum allowable population, what happens to the surplus?

There will come a time, supposing the poachers are kept at bay, when Ngare Sergoi is at its premium carrying capacity, just as has been reached in some South African reserves. The answer to this problem is three-fold: the surplus rhinos can be moved to another reserve or area of bush to establish another population; they can be sent to ranches; or they can be culled.

The number of reserves and locations are finite, so it would seem as if we may well reach the stage where culling of captive or specialist reserve-bred animals is meritable. In South Africa, both black and white rhinos are culled.

This causes a furore in conservation circles. South Africa has a surfeit whilst the other African countries are losing or have lost all their rhinos. Why not, some argue, give excess rhinos to these other countries? There are two reasons why this was not done in the past. First, African countries have been loath to deal with apartheid-centred South Africa, and secondly, the South African game authorities have been reluctant to ship their rhinos out, only to have them poached within months. Or sooner. It has not been unknown for a rhino in transit by road to be hijacked by poachers and killed long before it even arrived at its destination.

Translocating rhinos from areas threatened by poachers to safer havens, as described in Chapter 11, is also an option for conservationists. It was, when first mooted, a revolutionary idea but has proved to be remarkably effective and is now a widespread practice.

Another idea is that of game management areas (GMAs).

Put simply, these are large areas of bush which adjoin national parks or reserves and may have some human habitation in them. These areas act as buffers between the national park and surrounding human occupation areas of farm- or tribal land. In the game management areas, controlled hunting is permitted. Local people are able to apply for and obtain licences letting them hunt for smaller game. This process goes some of the way towards alleviating the pressures upon the reserve and puts a halt to much of the subsistence poaching activity. Of course, big game may not be shot in the GMA land and the poachers will still operate here.

Whereas the GMAs are a sort of cross between a game ranch and a reserve, in that the game is utilised under supervision, the integrated development project goes one step further.

This is an ingenious idea and is, I believe the ultimate answer to conservation.

Put simply, it operates like this: within a defined area, the local people are educated into understanding that the game and the habitat is their responsibility. They will be encouraged to protect it by not hunting it (save under GMA-type rules), not clearing it using the slash-and-burn method and not molesting it. In return they will receive a percentage of the income of that land which is put into community development – a school or clinic, say. However, for every instance of environmental damage, for every poached carcass discovered, a percentage of that income is withheld.

In this way, the local people realise that the bush is theirs to husband. Poaching becomes an anti-social activity as does habitat denigration. Rangers, instead of hunting poachers, go out to keep a check on wildlife stocks and search for any dead animals, checking that they died of natural causes.

To make such a scheme successful a structure must exist whereby that area of bush does produce an income: this will be dealt with later.

The public awareness of the plight of wildlife – and rhinos in particular – is an important part of conservation and protection but I believe it is largely ineffectual and too much money is spent upon maintaining it. To advertise the rhino's predicament in the West is to preach to the converted. Nebulous friends-of-rhinos societies and mass mailings of save-the-rhino car-bumper stickers and brochures do not radically help the rhino, unless a vast proportion of the money gained is applied directly to the problem of conservation rather than to the furtherance of the fund-raising body. In my opinion, money would be far better spent in the bush, buying equipment, increasing conservation man-power, improving the infrastructure of the anti-poaching system and – most importantly – putting a value on the wildlife in the eyes of local people, making the animals more viable as ongoing, renewable resources, whose continued presence may directly and positively benefit them.

Fund-raising to maintain a conservation or protectionist infrastructure is, I believe, just a short term panacea rather than a lasting cure of the whole disease.

I often wonder if it would not be better to use the money to pay local subsistence and franchised poachers not to poach rather than pay a handicapped police force to try and prevent them. The two poachers in handcuffs were not seeking to own a Mercedes Benz: they just wanted to live and be comfortable in the way of life they saw as traditional and important to them.

Of course, there are inter-governmental agencies, accords and treaties that try to regulate the business of wild animal products, be they live creatures or trophies and bits of them.

The mainstay of this regulation is CITES – the Convention on International Trade in Endangered Species. Many countries are signatories to this convention which, to a point, has been successful in counteracting much of the trade in animals and products. However, it is not legally binding, and just because a country signs to uphold the convention does not mean an end to poaching. Corruption, national maladministration, inefficient policing, low fiscal support and sheer apathy often foil the intentions. It is true that, under CITES, the activities of *djambia* makers have been severely curtailed, ivory trading has been placed under a moratorium and rhino horns are internationally regarded as illicit goods. But this has not saved the rhino or the elephant.

China, South Korea, Taiwan (which is not a CITES signatory country) and Thailand have failed to stop rhino horn and products importation. Press and media campaigns by such bodies as the World-Wide Fund for Nature (WWF) are all very well, but they do not strike at the root of the problem.

When talking, treaties, agreements, diplomacy and reason fail, I do not see why open warfare should not be joined. I do not agree with the attitude that it is difficult to reconcile wildlife conservation with the spilling of human blood. Between 1985 and 1987, Zimbabwe rangers killed 27 poachers: the poachers had killed well over 200 rhinos, thus damaging not only the long-term local black rhino population but also their long-term habitat, to the detriment of all the other resident animals and humans.

The rhino has little chance of protection when one considers that even the flagship animal of the WWF, the panda, is still being illegally killed. I know of a friend travelling in China in 1990 who was offered a panda pelt for US$5000.

So much for CITES. The convention has no teeth. It is merely a piece of paper which cannot be legally enforced in an international court. Even within the European Economic Community (EEC) where laws do exist to redress this considerable anomaly, the legal structure is hazy and inefficient and lacks co-ordination or dedication."CITES is little more than a WWF brochure begging support but unable to demand it."

In the meantime, prices of rhino products are rising, spurred on by the rhino's increasing scarcity. In the spring of 1990, my enquiries in Hong Kong showed that the cost of a whole black rhino horn had risen by about 60 per cent over the previous two years. No traditional medicine dealer whom I visited was without horn and other rhino products and many said that they had ample supplies to last 'a long time'. This is not surprising as the dosage is small. Despite not currently buying horn, most were raising their prices on medicinal sales in keeping with the inflation in the raw material costs. However, I also discovered, to my dismay, that a number of Hong Kong Chinese were investing in rhino horn against the day when the animal was extinct.

The terrible thing is that, when all is said and done, the trade in rhino horn is beginning to diminish but not because of conservation measures, successful legislation, international diplomacy, publicity drives, wildlife charities' fund-raising and public awareness campaigns, changes in traditional medicine usage and international pressures. It is slowing simply because there are now too few rhinos to sustain the market at its previous rate. Trade is dying out because the rhino is dying out.

It is imperative that the conservation of rhinos undergoes a radical and immediate change of direction. Quite clearly, all the methods given in this chapter have proved to be either ultimately useless or of use only in regional localities, and have not been going long enough for their true effectiveness to be assessed. If they were all effective, there would still be large populations of wild rhinos roaming the bush of sub-Saharan Africa.

LICENSED TO KILL,
LICENSED TO CONSERVE

H UNTING big game was not all glamour and thrill as Chapter 8 might imply, although the safari was based upon the premise that if one paid to hunt in Africa, one was in for a time of considerable and unforgettable excitement. In the heyday of the big-game shooting safari, in the years between the two world wars and again up until the mid-1950s, there was no greater adventure to be had on earth save perhaps, in the exploration of new lands, than to go into the bush with a white hunter.

The phrase 'white hunter' is a curious one. It simply means a white man hunting as opposed to a black man, and yet it has about it an aura for which many film stars would gladly pay. The white hunter is seen, even today when the breed is almost as extinct as some of the creatures they hunted, as a handsome man of near superhuman abilities – a crack shot, a man of steel nerves and lightning reflexes, physically strong in a lean way with the heightened senses of a gazelle and a knowledge of bushcraft rivalled only by the bushman himself. He was also, by the way, a good cook over an open fire, able to drive a safari car over rough terrain for hours on end, could butcher and skin an animal to perfection, could speak a large number of native dialects and was a prodigious, skilful, gentle, aware and resourceful lover with the stamina of a bull rhino. (Many white hunters of the old school will sincerely attest to the fact that the most dangerous animal on any safari was the client's wife: saving that, a single woman was the next most dangerous. J.A. Hunter once had a female client who attempted to commit suicide by running at two rhinos, attempting to provoke a charge. By a mixture of quick thinking and sheer good luck, Hunter saved her from herself and the irate rhinos.)

In truth, many of them did match up to at least 75 per cent of the claims put against them. They were and are – the few who still exist, like Charles Cottar's grand- and great-grandson – men more than a cut above the rest. They have the life of the bush in their veins and are uncomfortable in cities, stone houses and offices.

Today, they hunt far less, safaris being more photographic or adventure expeditions that shooting trips.

Despite the hunting (and therefore killing) aspects of their lives, they were and are essential to the future of the bush and all its wildlife. This is not a recent development but one that has existed since the turn of the century when they saw where the future lay.

For many of the white hunters, exploration and their own private safaris (without clients) went hand in hand. In the first half of the Twenties Charles Cottar, for example, travelled far into what is today Zaïre, hunting elephant, and he was without doubt the first white man to visit the area, well ahead even of the missionaries and the early cartographers. He also walked or rode far into the Northern Frontier Province of Kenya and explored large areas of unmapped Tanganyika within months of the country coming under British protection: it had previously been German East Africa.

Charles Cottar is typical of the early white hunter. In common with the rest of his kind, he lived by hunting. He shot for his own food and for the mouths of the few Africans he took with him: he traded in ivory and skins. He also shot for sport which had been the reason for his leaving his native America and settling in what was then called British East Africa. He tried farming but this was never truly successful and he was obliged, not against his will, to earn from the bush.

In this, he was only doing what the African native – and peasants throughout the world – had done for years. He made his living out of nature's bounty which seemed, at the time, endless. Like the poachers I met, these early men could see no end to Mother Nature's provision of game.

In time, not only personal hunting was lucrative but so was taking others out to hunt. This was how the safari business, which in one form or another is the mainstay of modern African tourism, came about. The commercial safari was born.

Not all white hunters were necessarily moral hunters. They were never deliberately cruel, had enormous respect for their quarry and were bound by an unwritten code of natural justice. But it must also be said, however, that some of them poached. This is not to say that they operated as today's poachers do, killing at random. Poaching in the 'old days' did not mean annihilating a species, but hunting without a licence having been paid to the authorities.

All animals were licensed according to their size, 'fame' as big game, population numbers and market value – that is, the value of their products. A hunter bought a game licence which would allow him to kill and (if he wished) sell a certain number of each animal listed on his licence. In 1913, for example, a standard game licence in Kenya cost £50 and allowed the holder to shoot (or capture) two elephants, two rhinos, two hippos, two zebra, one buffalo and two hundred gazelle, antelope and smaller game. The shooting of lions and leopards was unrestricted, because it was deemed there were so many of them that they were classed as vermin. With hindsight, this was a major ecological error: the removal of so many main predators, which had reached not verminous but natural population levels, was to herald the start of the imbalance of the bush.

Revenue from game licences was not ploughed back into the administration of the bush. It either paid for the administration of the licence system or it entered the general coffers of the government. This trend, which has continued in most African countries until very recently, was wrong. It was like taking the earnings of a shop and putting them into a private bank account without buying more stock for the shelves.

The hunters' respect for their quarry was often to put them at odds with their clients. I have met a number of white hunters whose contempt for their customers was, at times, extreme.

Many clients were rich enough to pay for anything, and there was a degree of sycophancy exhibited by some hunters towards them. Many hunters regretted this and some took pains to see that it did not occur to compromise their attitudes towards the wildlife. Yet there were other hunters, it must be said, for whom the purse was sometimes more important than the principles of good game management and use.

Most white hunters were conservationists in embryo. This concept is hard to understand today when hunting has taken on the cachet of deliberate destruction, the opinion no doubt enhanced when one considers that the hunters were also frequently licensed by the colonial authorities specifically to shoot out certain species. J.A. Hunter, for example, reduced the local rhino population by over 80 per cent in the Kamba tribal area: it has never recovered although there are still some rhino remaining and breeding.

It would be unwise of me to give the location of these rhinos: even the local Africans are protective of them which I find to be a most encouraging development. I know of two black rhinos which live on a sisal farm. The owner of the farm is keen to keep them. They do no harm whatsoever to the crops, do not raid the farm-workers' *shambas* (smallholdings) and are rarely seen, so are therefore of no danger to the men working in the sisal blocks. The rhinos live in the dense patches of scrub that remain on the farm (which is some hundreds of hectares in area), drinking at night from the irrigation channels and bore-holes and wallowing in muddy areas unsuitable for cultivation. If only more farms and farmers would be so accommodating, but on a larger scale, in order to allow viable breeding populations to exist.

Today, the term white hunter does not necessarily refer to a gun-carrying white man. He is more likely to be carrying a bush knife and a rifle for protection, not so much from wild animal attack but from the uncertainties of meeting gangs of *shifta* bandits: even in the heydays of the safari before the Second World War, the shooting of animals in defence was a fairly rare occurrence. When he points his clients' attention it is with a camera not a telescope rifle sight.

Modern hunters are aware that without wildlife they would have no income. Even today, when hunting throughout the birthplace of the safari – Kenya – is forbidden, hunters make a living from game by taking out photographers and film-makers.

It follows, therefore, that hunters must be conservationists in order to maintain their livelihood and many are heavily involved in the protection of habitat and wildlife.

This is not new.

Selous, writing in his memoirs,[1] states that he believes the problem with the Boer farmers and hunters was that they did not understand or appreciate their quarry, and did not seek to develop any natural history or scientific knowledge about the animals. Most hunters today have a wealth of scientific data at their fingertips and this has become the name of their game. They must have this kind of wisdom if the bush they love is to survive.

I am not implying that only hunters were conservationists. As long ago as 1900, the high commissioner for Uganda, Harry Johnston, espoused what has today become the central aspect of bush protection. He declared that foreign hunters, by which he meant

181

white men, were one of the greatest blots of civilisation, and he suggested that hunting with a gun should be replaced by hunting with a camera. He was sixty years ahead of his time in thinking and was thoroughly unpopular with many for his outrageous opinions. He was not only critical of hunters but pleased by their downfall. When a German hunter called Kolb was killed by a black rhino (having shot over 150 rhinos in three years), Johnston remarked that the death was deserved, adding that he considered each of the dead rhinos to be a far more interesting mammal than the hunter.

I admit to being in complete accord with Johnston's proposition, but I also accept that hunting has a place in conservation.

What the general public cannot understand today, in the light of man's rape of the planet, is the relationship between modern hunting and that of the past, and the relationship between hunting and conservation.

While I consider killing for sport a pointless and immature activity, I do accept that there are people who need to shoot, and I see no moral objection to this – but with several provisos.

When Roosevelt went out to Africa to massacre wildlife 'in the name of science', he paid US$85 per elephant, and US$15 per rhino or hippo. At that time, the cash worth of rhino horn was about 60 East African shillings per kilo. (The value was also assessed in other currencies: Arab slavers operating in Ethiopia considered a rhino horn equal in value to four able men.)

Assuming a primary horn to weigh - for the sake of argument - 7 kilos, then each rhino would have been worth to Roosevelt or a contemporary hunter between 400–600 shillings with both horns on the market. At the time, 20 EAsh was about equal to one dollar. This was a substantial return on a small outlay with a 100 per cent profit on a small specimen. Bigger rhinos would have made much bigger financial returns.

It is obvious that the hunter clients were cheating the bush of its value in much the same fashion, if not to such an extent, as the modern poacher does.

My first proviso is, therefore, that hunters pay a going rate for their 'fun'.

At the turn of the century, rhinos were plentiful: the black rhino population of Kenya was estimated to be in excess of 150,000. Even at the end of the 1960s, the population stood at around 20,000. Today, that population is reduced to just a few hundreds. It is, therefore, impossible to allow rhino hunting in East Africa. However, in some places, rhinos are abundant for the habitat provided. In South Africa, where conservation is highly regarded and very successful, both black and white rhino areas are reaching carrying capacity and the shooting of rhinos occurs from time to time as part of a process of culling.

As I have mentioned, these 'excess' rhinos have two possible fates. First, they could be translocated to other suitable habitats but South African game authorities are sometimes reluctant to do this. However, a second alternative is to let a hunter in and charge him to shoot those rhinos that are surplus to requirements, as it were.

Under these controls, only a specific individual animal would be killed. The hunter's desire would be sated. He should not, in my opinion, be allowed to keep the trophy: let him be photographed with his handiwork but let the horns, hide, and other marketable products be retained for commercial sale.

The price that one might place upon such an animal would vary, but I would think it reasonable to charge substantially high sums for the 'privilege' of killing it. And there are those who would pay handsomely for such an opportunity, no matter how distasteful this might seem to many others.

The next stipulation is that all the money raised – from the shooting permission, the sale of the carcass and so on – be used exclusively for conservation, for the purchase of other areas of bush, for scientific research, for the protection of wildlife and to provide an income for local people who will then see that wildlife is of value to them.

It is here that the crux of the matter lies.

It is hard for Westerners to do, but I suggest we must put ourselves into the shoes of the bush African. His life is conducted at poverty level. He has little to alleviate this – no industry and no way by which to make a living: unless he poaches and destroys habitat, he cannot even revert to his traditional meagre bush life.

He stands outside a game park or reserve and looks in. There are animals there – meat, skins, money. He cannot get at them unless he risks imprisonment or being shot. He sees rich tourists visiting the animals, riding in luxury vehicles, eating well in the game lodges, wearing clothes and wristwatches and gold rings, carrying cameras worth several years' of his income. They are spending a lot of their money to see those animals.

183

The bush African sees none of this income. It goes into the pockets of central government, of tour operators and hoteliers.

It is small wonder that the African is jealous of the animals and the tourist for his wealth because he sees none of it.

The answer is that the local native must get a return on wildlife. Not just one man who poaches having a three-month holiday at the expense of a rhino or two. The whole community must benefit. This does not remove the native's *modus vivendi* or affect the traditional way of life: if anything, it brings it into the modern economic culture. His controlled use of wildlife is, after all, what he has been doing for centuries: with scientific assistance and the monitoring of animals to be killed, avoiding haphazard killing, the use of wild animals can be sustained as a renewable resource, properly husbanded.

Take a rhino in a patch of thorn scrub. The African knows it is worth so many shillings or *kwacha* to him. He kills it, the resource is removed but he has some money. If the rhino remains alive, visited by tourists, it still earns money, but not for the villager.

Conservation must accept that if it is to work and wildlife is to survive, then it must be shown to benefit the locals.

I suggest this is done in several ways.

First, all game and wildlife tourism should be specifically taxed, and the revenues directed specifically at local populations. Secondly, all profits from such should be divided between the tour operator and the wildlife authorities. Thirdly, more local people should be employed in wildlife tourism, management and support, paid for by the tour operator as well as local authorities. Fourthly, the wildlife should be utilised where this might be allowed where population numbers are in excess.

In principle, there is nothing wrong with humanely killing a rhino any more than a domestic animal. Indeed, a rhino shot humanely in the bush, where it has lived out its natural life in its natural manner, is far better off than a cow being driven to the abattoir.

If the rhino existed in such numbers as to allow it to be utilised, it could earn large sums of money in a regulated market.

Consider what just one horn could earn for a local African economy: one good-size horn could build and equip a clinic or construct a school and pay for its teachers for a year.

— 15 —

DAWN OR DARKNESS

How can money be made out of wildlife other than by the sale of printed tea-towels and plastic beakers by the wildlife charity organisations? The answer lies in a good many different directions, all of which must be addressed if wildlife – and particularly the rhino and other 'spectacular' animals – is to be saved.

Before considering the options, it is important to ask why money should be made out of wild animals and their habitats at all.

The answer to this is simple: because of the way we have constructed the world to operate, wildlife must have an economic value to make it viable and keep it worthwhile. It is not enough to say that the African bush and wildlife must be preserved for its own sake, for aesthetic or moral reasons.

I say *preserve* rather than *conserve* for the former is the approach being taken at present and which is doing the most harm. To preserve something is to keep it safe and untouched, like a museum specimen. Roman vases on shelves are preserved: they are looked at but they are never used, seldom touched and have an artificial value placed upon them. What wildlife charity organisations would do is the same thing: preserve game so that it might be looked at but never touched, never used as it was in the past and artificially valued according to its uniqueness.

This attitude is what has led to the farcical situation that has existed (and still does in a few places) of having individual rhinos protected by their own armed escorts who live with them in the bush on a 24-hour basis, guarding them as a warden guards a prisoner. Such a rhino, permanently shadowed by a human, is not living in a natural state: it is, for all intents and purposes, little more than a zoo animal without a surrounding cage of bars. Indeed, many

185

of these highly protected rhinos do end up behind bars: at night, in order to guard them effectively, they are driven (or wander of their own accord, so habituated have they become) into a stout enclosure where they are watched over through the darkness.

The rhino's uniqueness is a problem, too. The more rare something becomes – like rhino horn or ivory – the more it will be coveted and the more valuable and worthwhile stealing it becomes. Poachers are, after all, thieves.

What is required is that it be conserved: in other words, protected like the Roman vase, stored and nurtured and looked at with wonderment but it must also be used, its value realised. It must have a viability not only because of its rarity but also because of its usefulness. The museum exhibits are dead and sterile: wildlife cannot be allowed to go that way.

Western nations may consider the wildness of the African nature reserve to be wonderful, essential and beautiful, but to the local African, hungry and poor, it is not a fascinating landscape but a bit of earth – and *his* country – he would like to plant maize on, graze his cattle or goats on and make a living from it, just as his ancestors did.

For many Africans, the game reserves are much-needed land being refused to them not by their own governments necessarily but by foreigners who have made a policy and moral decision not to let them on it. Often, the reasons for this exclusion are not given and, in fairness, if they were they would often not be understood.

This exclusion causes a good deal of resentment between local people and the reserve/conservation authorities – and the wildlife. Subsistence and franchised poaching occurs not only as a means of earning money but also, in some countries, as a means of getting back at the authorities and their attitudes. For example, subsistence poaching occurs quite widely in Kenya. As Kenya has one of the highest standards of living in sub-Saharan Africa, one has to question the motivation behind the killing. Indeed, in Kenya, part of the *raison d'être* of the *shifta* bandits infiltrating from Somalia is to disrupt local societies and, thereby, destabilise the central government.

Furthermore, in Kenya as elsewhere, animals are killed as a way of making a political point. In early 1990, one of the very few rhinos left in the Masai Mara was killed for exactly that reason. It was not even poached but bluntly murdered, the horn not removed. The carcass was not hidden but left in full view for the rangers to

186

discover, a poignant and very powerful message.

There is an understandable animosity in the minds of many Africans – game parks are unnecessary. A game park of, say, fifteen thousand square kilometres could employ several hundred people in the roles of rangers, administration officers, safari camp and tourist infrastructure staff and labourers. The same land area could support many times that number if humans lived on it.

Those employed in the game park earn money from tourism alone and are therefore vulnerable, at the whim of foreign economies for, if times are hard in Europe, the tourists fail to come. Whatever money these people do earn goes into the local economy – up to a point. Game park entrance fees go to the national government and all profits from tourism follow them except, of course, for that substantial percentage which goes into the accounts of the tour operators, the foreign airlines and holiday companies.

Wildlife – not just the rhino – and the wild habitat are very valuable.

People will pay to visit and photograph the animals, to walk in the danger of the bush and, nowadays, to take adventure safaris in it: I have rafted down the hippo- and crocodile-packed Athi river on a rubber boat (which was, without doubt, one of the most exhilarating, foolish, dangerous and downright stupid things I have ever done) and I know of other rafting companies in Kenya who offer similar thrills on the Tana river; another company offers mountain biking up Mount Kilimanjaro.

The animals which are the major earners are the Big Five and, of these, the rhino, elephant and lion are those most tourists want to see. Why? Because the lion is the mythical king of the beasts, a symbol of power, strength, vitality and violence. The rhino and elephant are sought after because they are unique and under threat.

The rhino is the flagship of the bush. Publicity in recent years has justifiably highlighted its plight and placed it as the African equivalent of the panda, in the most-at-risk brigade. Its attraction is increased because it is one major animal the tourist is least likely to see. I have overheard a group of eight tourists in the Masai Mara offer their minibus driver US$200 if he could show them a rhino. Tips for a lion would not exceed US$40. Even at gratuity level, the rhino is worth a small fortune to the local African.

It is, in my opinion, the main possible money earner alongside the elephant.

Poachers prove this point: these are the two animals most killed for the value of their horn or tusks.

However, the earning capacity does not rest with tourists who take their pictures and buy a few native carvings. Indeed, the photographic trophy is the cheapest available. Consider the following package offered as a photographic safari:

An economy bush safari in authentic style, with a difference . . . It is more likely to appeal to those who would rather listen to a lion roaring close by than be with two hundred people or so in a lodge. For transport we use trail blazing 18 seater, 1000 mile fuel range four wheel drive specially converted 9 ton Mercedes trucks, carrying complete camping equipment, all necessary fresh and frozen food and our own fresh water. Your safari escort gives nightly talks around the camp fire about the day's flora and fauna and what to expect the next day. With bush camping the whole safari is one long game run . . .

This sounds excellent and no doubt it is superb value for money: having seen the itinerary for this safari, offered by a leading package operator, I can be certain that clients will see elephants and have a very good chance of encountering rhinos, lions and even cheetahs. This safari costs, at the peak rate, only £1049 (US$2000) per person for fourteen nights, eight of which are spent in the bush on full board and six in a good quality hotel on the Kenyan coast at half board. And that includes a return air fare from London.

I suggest in this case that the rhino, its fellow animals, its habitats and those Africans who may not share it are getting short-changed in no uncertain fashion, and that the rhino is not earning its full potential.

How else might the bush earn money?

The answer is by utilising it.

Copper, gold, diamonds – these are the mainstays of some African economies and they will die out one day. Frantic searches are being made for new geological wealth: there may well be oil in Zambia, underneath the South Luangwa National Park. In time, this too will run out.

What will not die out, if properly managed, is the wildlife. The bush provides one of Africa's few sustainable and, more importantly, renewable resources.

188

In other words, the animals must be used just as cows and pigs and chickens are used. The glory is that the wild animals will not spend their lives wintering in barns, mouldering in pig units or pecking each other in boredom in a battery shed, never seeing the light of day and being fed hormones and the recycled waste of their ancestors.

An example of how the bush might work – and, I believe, its only chance of salvation – lies in game ranching.

Take a large area of bush and let it develop naturally. Maintain it. See that predators do not increase in large numbers, see that no species overruns another. Management is the secret.

At the Ndumu National Park in northern Natal, I attended a night cull of nyala[1]. This game reserve, especially being used for both black and white rhino breeding, has had all of its hyena shot out to protect rhino calves. Furthermore, there are no lions in the park and not many leopards. The result is a burgeoning herbivore population safe from predation.

The nyala is a large antelope, the bull animal not dissimilar in looks from a kudu. The carrying capacity of Ndumu was, I was told, about 2000 animals. The population was nearer 5000 when I was there. The answer was to control by culling. These animals were not, however, simply shot and burned, as many conservationists would prefer.

On one night, I watched just over 100 nyala die each with a single shot through the head fired by a game ranger at close range from a vehicle, using either a night-sight or a hunting lamp. Not one nyala suffered: not one animal had to be shot twice. The cost of each animal was the price of the bullet – say US$1. In the early hours, the animals were butchered and skinned. The offal (much sought after by local Africans as a delicacy) was given away to the butchery staff. The hides were sent for tanning. The meat was hung in strips in a drying shed to be made into biltong. All these products were sold and earned money for the upkeep of the reserve.

Indeed, a comfortable profit was made but not just in cash terms. The profit was shared by nearly 100 rhinos, a fabulous bird-life, a wide variety of other herbivores, hippos and crocodiles in the pans and even wild tortoises.

Hunting under controlled conditions maintains the *status quo*, the natural balance and provides safety for the rhinos. No poaching occurs in the park: there is no need, for the local Africans see its

189

value. This is sadly not the case in other parts of South Africa where, since the abolition of apartheid, Africans are starting to demand game reserve land, traditionally theirs, be returned to them. Such a demand, made from ignorance, will be their undoing if their wishes are complied with: they will go the way of the rest of Africa, losing that which is their best resource. And the animals will lose out, too.

Due to pressure from conservation organisations, from CITES and from similar bodies, a vast amount of game, which could otherwise be turned into cash resources for wildlife, is destroyed.

The fact that culling goes on is conveniently ignored by conservation societies. It is counterproductive to their message to inform their members that animals are controlled. For the last thirty years, wildlife charities have misled public opinion by fostering uninformed public emotion to raise money that sustains the charity itself as much as it does wildlife. Out of the glare of publicity, they have fully accepted supportable management practices yet they have withheld such controversial matters from the public domain.

The supposedly unpleasant realities of game conservation – utilisation, population controls, culling – have been kept secret and the public has no concept of what necessarily goes on.

Instead, a blind eye is turned by these wildlife administrations and organisations and the marketing of such products is refused, thus stripping game and reserve authorities from fully realising their assets. It must be remembered that, in South Africa for example, the universally protected elephant is culled now, for the sake of population control. Conservation has been so successful that numbers are too great. Yet the ivory obtained from these essential cullings cannot be sold as the international market has been banned. A main source of conservation funding has been outlawed by the conservation charities and lobby groups.

Earlier in this book, I mentioned game ranching where an area of bush becomes a wild 'farm' from which the owner takes animals under controlled circumstances. The idea of wildlife farming is one that needs much expansion.

I have visited a crocodile farm in Africa. The reptiles are bred in huge pools from eggs laid by a small breeding group of enormous crocodiles up to 5 metres long and weighing close on 1000 kgs. The eggs, incubated artificially, obtain a hatch rate over 400 per cent better than might be achieved in the wild. Controlling the temperature also decides the sex of the hatchlings so there is never an imbalance. The farm kills the crocodiles at a certain age and the skins sell into the European leather trade. However, the farm breeds more crocodiles than it needs so it has already taken part in re-stocking many central African rivers where poachers had wiped the animal out. Because the croc-skin trade is fully regulated, no poaching occurs because skins may only be traded through accredited dealers and European leather firms will only deal with accredited sources.

The farm is a conservation success. No crocodiles are taken from the wild: wild habitats are restocked when needed. Trade is maintained and poaching no longer viable. The natives who live around the farm are employed there and it is a major (indeed, the only!) local industry bringing in good economic return. Everyone wins.

What if we could farm rhinos like crocodiles? I see no reason why we should not. They are easily kept in semi-captivity – look at the safari parks of Europe and America. Their product (the horn) is all the people really want so why not keep them on a farm and periodically de-horn them? As a primary horn grows at the rate of about 12 cm. per annum, each rhino could produce at least one sizeable horn every three years, earning thousands of dollars each time. By-products like dung and urine could also be sold, maintaining a small business during the horn-growing periods.

If there was a legalised trade, the rhino would survive and the Far Eastern traditional medicine dealer would have his supply. As numbers increased, as they would under breeding control, more could be released into the wild. Again, everyone would win. The only thing that prevents this concept is the embargo on rhino products and the failure to allow and establish a legalised market.

Taken to its extreme, this idea could be applied to many animals. It is only scientifically doing what Africans have been doing for centuries – carefully living off the land and its bounty which they have sustained.

The greatest source of income from wildlife comes not from putting it on show but from utilisation, and one of the main aspects of this is commercial, licensed hunting.

It is interesting to see what happens when big game hunting is stopped. Until 1977, the government of Kenya allowed hunting under licence: then, under international pressure, hunting was banned. The hunters who had had a vested interest in maintaining habitat, the wellbeing of the various species from which they could earn money and that of all the other animals interrelated to them, were excluded from the system. Furthermore, as the hunters had been a main source for the training of game rangers and wildlife wardens, the system lost its primary educative input. Farmers were still allowed to kill game that affected their crops: previously, many had allowed for this depredation of their harvests because the animals could be hunted and the money obtained from them would make up for the loss. With hunting banned, there was no economic reason to keep wildlife on farms and no way of recouping losses: it was shot out.

In Kenya, under a concessionary system, local natives received a percentage of hunting licence revenues thus giving them a vested interest in the wildlife of their area. This disappeared with the ban and subsistence poaching increased severalfold to make up the shortfall and because there was no longer a reason to protect the game. The hunting ban pitted wildlife against the people.

Hunters operating in an area were also a substantial deterrent to the big-time commercial poachers of rhino and elephant. As soon as hunters disappeared, so did the game they had conserved.

A foreign hunter from the developed world does not just sit in a minibus or safari car and pay package holiday rates. He has to meet considerable extra expense.

First, there is the actual hunting licence which these days is justifiably expensive: fortunately gone are the days, as in 1934, when a special rhino licence in East Africa cost £5. In 1967, when rhinos could still be hunted in Kenya, a rhino cost £100 which was little more, in real terms than it had cost thirty years previously.

Today, the cost of a hunting licence (where hunting is permitted) can be as high as £3500 and still exclude very many species. Secondly, the hunter has to pay for the exclusive hire of vehicles (more than one for there is passenger as well as camping equipment to transport), drivers and repair staff. Thirdly, he has to employ camp staff – tent boys, cooks, domestics, laundrymen – and bush staff such as a tracker, several butchers and, if his licence allows for trophy taking (which some do not), someone who can skin and prepare his trophies. Fourthly, he has to employ a white hunter or guide. Fifthly, he has to pay export permits for whatever he wishes to retain.

Prices are, of course, relative, but it is a fair assumption to say that the income derived from one week's hunting safari is approximately equal to that obtained from over 200 photographic tourists. If one adds to the licence a much-sought-after animal such as a lion, an elephant – or even a rhino – the income is considerably increased.

How much is a rhino worth?

The black rhino is the most valuable trophy in Africa, not only to the hunter but also to zoos. It is a rare creature and therefore commands a high price, dead or alive. The white rhino is perhaps the next most valuable.

Properly managed, the rhino can be bred in the wild with success: the population at Ndumu and many other places proves it. So long as the negative factors in their environment are controlled, breeding patterns are good. All that is needed to optimise rhino numbers is a suitable habitat, adequate permanent water sources, the eradication of commercial poaching, the control of hyena numbers and the maintenance of the population at about sixty per cent of carrying capacity. Research shows that productivity drops when the rhino population of a given area is less than twenty-five or more than seventy-five per cent of its carrying capacity. Populations may be maintained at healthy numbers by translocation or by shooting.

The success of the conservation of the white rhino shows what sound management can achieve. Half a century ago, fewer than fifty white rhinos were left in Umfolozi but, due to Player's translocation and conservation programme, they are today so plentiful that they have to be closely controlled to maintain breeding capacity on the land and stop them, putting it simply, eating themselves out of house and home. Rhinos from here have been translocated all over the world and to other South African reserves and game ranches.

In the Pilanesburg National Park, South Africa's third biggest reserve which was, for some years, administered by Ron Thomson, up to ten white rhinos a year are shot by hunters: it is often difficult to find homes for non-trophy animals in a burgeoning population.

Those which are hunted as trophies sell for up to US$15,000 each, occasionally even more: this is how much a hunter will pay to shoot *just one rhino*. The white rhino is, therefore, more valuable than any domestic stock. Its utilisation, arising from the success of management and husbandry – which might be termed the farming of the bush habitat – is a major source of wildlife financing.

193

If a rhino could be shot for this much money in, say, impover-ished Zambia, and some of the money put back into the local enonomy rather than the national one, the need for poaching would cease. A local human population would understand the value of the rhinos and far from poaching them would protect them. Poaching would be a strongly anti-social activity.

I should like to see some rhino translocated into the South Luangwa National Park: the local people would see them and be told to guard them. Initially, they would be paid to do so (by a Western wildlife charity, perhaps?) but, in time, they would be allowed to let a rich hunter in to shoot one, perhaps two. As time went by, the stock would climb to breeding capacity, the poaching would reduce then cease because the local people would be earning money from wildlife, the rhino would be safe in an area where it is now all but extinct but where it was numerous twenty-five years ago, and the local people would be better off financially and materially.

In some places, where conservation has saved a habitat, even if the larger and spectacular animals like rhino have disappeared and have not yet been translocated back in, there is still room for limited shooting. Several rangers in Kenya have told me that they could raise considerable revenues for game parks just by arranging bird shoots. As one of them said, it is one thing to shoot driven semi-tame pheasants flying through an English wood towards the guns ahead of a line of beaters (a 'sport' I find both boring and unjust) and quite another to shoot francolin by walking them up in the African bush when turning a corner might bring the shooter face to face not with a fox but a leopard. What is more, far more people shoot game birds than would want to shoot large mammals.

Any hunting must be strictly controlled. It is not just a case of paying for a rhino, trekking out into the bush and shooting one, as in the old days of big-game hunting. The individual animal must be marked – it is old and at the end of its genetically useful life, it is sterile, or it is surplus to the number best suited for that specific habitat. In other words, it is an animal that the authorities would soon cull or nature kill in its own way.

I see no moral objection to having rich hunters do the job of the rangers and pay heavily for it. The nyala cull I attended could have earned a substantial amount of foreign currency if a hunter had been charged to join in with the 'enjoyment' of necessary killing.

There are places where rhinos are over-numerous. They should be put to good use, for the benefit of their species and the bush.

As I have said, I have no desire to kill a rhino whatsoever. But I accept that they have to be culled and if someone will pay heavily for this then let him do so.

The point is this: when conservation becomes successful, as it has in a number of places, then killing must come in. The aim, therefore, must ultimately be to have conservation being so successful that it can sustain properly controlled utilisation. The important thing is that this does not evolve into the gratuitious, wasteful killing of the past.

What has to be protected against are past attitudes. A whole rethink of conservation, hunting and game utilisation has to be considered. What must not be allowed is what Carl Akeley called the old condition. In 1929, he visited the Tana river in Kenya where, just twenty years before, he had found vast numbers of rhino and buffalo: they were all gone, the buffalo herd at Theba reduced from 600 to sixty beasts. 'The unhappy remnant,' he wrote, 'of the magnificent fauna of Kenya now has its ear attuned to the rattle and bang of the motor car, which carries the alleged sportsman in his mad chase across the veldt in the hope of having the honour of killing the last of a given species.'

One of the greatest recent champions of the African rhino is Ron Thomson. He has dedicated his life to the protection and conservation of wild animals. Yet he is also a realist and he knows that, unless radical changes are made, the African rhino is utterly doomed. He wishes to see adequate bush management throughout Africa and, especially, he wants to see the black rhino – his favourite beast – managed properly.

His management options rub the wildlife charities up the wrong way, for he believes the rhino should be hunted. He puts his argument[2] as follows:

How can a man who has spent his life in the service of wildlife, particularly one who has caught and moved perhaps more black rhino than anyone else in the world, who has spent years researching their behaviour and ecology, and who was principally responsible for having the black rhino declared a 'Royal Game' animal back in the days when Zimbabwe was still Rhodesia, now propose that hunters should be allowed to shoot them: Especially at a time when they have already been poached to the brink of extinction in countries like Kenya and Tanzania . . .

It's easy. It's easy because I see hunting as the *only* means capable of arresting and reversing the poaching trend . . . and of giving [governments] the positive motivation to do something similarly constructive to counteract the poaching developments . . .

. . . And what about the black rhino's 'endangered' status? What about it? The black rhino, like several other species on the African continent has, in my considered opinion, achieved its 'endangered' status only because of man's inept management philosophies and the urbanised western world's pandering to uninformed, indoctrinated and emotional (but none-the-less genuine) attitudes to the sanctified idolatry of the wildlife resource.

'Shame. Those cruel hunters . . . and they call themselves sportsman?' Ad nauseam.

Such pious self-righteousness is destroying the wildlife resource. And if people don't like the idea of hunters killing 'little brown-eyed buck' they must not associate with hunters. They are entitled to their feelings and to their opinions, but they have no right to interfere in management processes that can save the continent's wildlife resource.

Ian Parker, in his fine book *The Ivory Crisis* states quite boldly (concerning the alleged plight of the *elephants* in Africa) that; 'The traditional 'villains' – the poachers and the ivory traders – are not as responsible for the plight of the elephants in many African countries as is generally alleged. The fault lies much more with the governments of these countries where game laws are outdated and corruption is commonplace: and with the international conservation bodies which, inept and inefficient as they often are, have much to answer for. No matter how good the cause they are serving, if there is an international ivory crisis it is the activities of the conservationists themselves which constitute the main danger to the survival of the elephant.' (And I might add, to many other species including the black rhino). 'The real crisis,' says Parker, 'is the current conservation philosophy.'

I have to agree with this summation: what applies to the still reasonably abundant elephant more than applies to the rhino. There is much wrong with wildlife management and until the problem is correctly addressed, there can be no safe future.

A reassessment of moral values and judgments is imperative. An understanding by non-Africans of the situation in Africa must be realised and wildlife must be regarded not through emotive but through reasoned eyes.

That these animal species and especially their homes must be saved, increased and coveted is vital. The method by which this is done must be re-aligned.

Another error of conservation thought lies in the enduring desire illustrated by many wildlife charities to protect entire species. This has not been successful with almost every large mammal to which this doctrine has been applied: if it had been efficacious, there would be a plentiful number of rhinos in Africa today. What the aim must be now, at this dire time, is not to seek to protect the entire species but to concentrate on conserving and expanding specific viable populations, consolidating effort and resources on maintaining cores of genetic wealth in appropriate habitats against such a time as they might be increased through future translocation or expansion of environment. It has to be said, however, that a few charities or individuals, such as Friends of Conservation with their work in the Masai Mara of Kenya and Anna Merz in her rhino sanctuary at Ngare Sergoi, are now adopting this approach. The sooner others follow their example, the better.

The downfall of the rhino is not the responsibility of black men with spears. It has come about by the impinging of white men's morals, attitudes, guns and greed. It is the white man who has brought about the collapse of African wildlife by implanting his rules on an environment to which he is unsuited. Animal and man co-existed quite happily, to the benefit of all, before Europeans arrived and upset the balance by over-killing, over-ploughing and over-utilising in ways that the land could not absorb.

I am reminded of an African government minister with whom I had dinner in Zambia. He was grateful I was taking an interest in conserving his wildlife: he saw this as redressing old colonial ills. Yet he complained, I believe with justification, about methodology.

'I am glad,' he said, 'you are here with your expertise and money to try and save our rhinos. But, you know, you have a bit of a cheek. You tell us we must save our wild creatures but where, in England, is the bear, is the wolf, is the wild pig? And the fox: it is hunted for no reason but to see pain. And the same for the big deer. Africans have never killed animals just to see them die but to use them – to eat them, to wear their skins. Maybe,' he allowed, 'as protection from them, too.'

His point is plainly made. We have ruined our national wild places and yet now we dictate to Africa to conserve theirs using our rules.

The future looks bleak. What must be achieved is massive. It is crucial that the encroachment of agriculture be reduced and existing farmlands and farming methods improved; the bush must earn more money through utilisation rather than exploitation, and there must be a decrease in human population. This latter, terribly, is a possibility: a number of conservation and game administration officials in Africa – both black and white men – to whom I have spoken are secretly of the opinion that AIDS may well save the bush.

Unless all these targets can be met – and very soon – the African rhino will hasten towards either extinction or being just a living equivalent of the Roman vase, standing in a museum field and being stared at until it dies.

EPILOGUE

Longleat Safari Park in Wiltshire has four resident white rhinos. They live in a vast ten-hectare meadow paddock with a few established deciduous trees, an area of bushes and a waterhole with muddy banks. With the exception of the visitors' tarmac road, the entire area is covered in deep, lush English grass. They share this arena with some eland and a number of camels. There is more than sufficient food for all.

The rhino group is divided into two bulls and two cows. Due to the territorial nature of rhinos, the two bulls have to be kept separated, so they live their life on a rota basis, three weeks on the grass and three in a large rhino stable separated into pens by very substantial steel bars.

At the end of three weeks, when the change-over occurs, the bull who is being released struts around the whole pasture, copiously urine-spraying and dunging. He is busy establishing his territory, eradicating the signs of his temporary predecessor and on the look-out for him should he appear.

They are watched over by a guardian tractor driven by a young man who spends his working life sitting in the cab, making sure they don't misbehave, head too close to visitors' cars or the perimeter fencing. If they do, a flat steel plate on the front gently nudges them out of trouble. The driver thinks his charges are quite wonderful and would love to see their wild relatives living in the bush.

At night, they are all housed in the stable where they are fed hay, coming in as readily as a dairy herd to the milking parlour as the light fades and the last visitors drive home. They are not brought indoors to protect them from the elements or from a fear of poachers but in order to be policed: left outside overnight, they

199

would be through the electric fencing and out into the countryside.

This nocturnal housing is the cause of some social friction amongst the four rhinos. The cows do not like one of the bulls and the two bulls must be kept in non-adjacent pens. Even so, they ram and snort at each other throughout the night. It must be very frustrating to live such a life at odds with the instinctive behaviour of the veldt.

Yet the rhinos show few ill-effects from their life of captivity. In the open they browse and rest as they would in the bush and they can readily cope with the weather of southern England. They have a wallow and a drinking pool and the grass is sufficiently rich that no food supplements are given to them. A vet visits them every Wednesday. They are very healthy, have no open wounds, no ticks (and no alarm-calling tick-birds), no intestinal parasites and no predators at all. They are pestered by flies in the summer but that is their only aggravation, and a drop of Optrex in their eyes relieves them. The neighbourhood poachers are intent on the farmer's pheasants, not the Marquis of Bath's rhinos: they do not enter the safari park for fear of finding themselves in the lions' or tigers' sections.

It would seem that these rhinos are happy. They ignore the visitors' cars just as they would if they were living in Nairobi National Park. One of the females has what a disciplinarian school-master might term a lively disposition – in other words, she stands no fools and will, from time to time, make it known to her guardian tractor that she is in control. The other cow lets the guardian tractor driver sit on her back when she's resting. That they have regularly bred with only one calf dying, the latest youngster being sent upon weaning back to South Africa to live in a private rhino sanctuary, is an indication of their contentment.

Certainly, they are captives. All around their vast paddock is a tall fence, more for keeping inquisitive people out than rhinos in. Gates prevent them joining other animals in their areas and heavy bars line their stable, keeping them from the Chapman's zebras next door as well as each other.

There are those people who, because these rhinos are captives, complain, who want them to be living free. They are not alone in this wish. The young man in the tractor would no doubt like to see them free, too. Yet they are not and they cannot be.

This is not for want of a shot of azaperone and an airline ticket.

There is not a free rhino in the world. They may not be hemmed in by actual fencing strung on poles (although this is just the case in many game parks, national reserves and ranches) but they are contained by farmland, cities, highways. There is no truly wild animal left on earth, just animals living their wild life in pockets of their original wilderness homes. There is no white rhino left on the face of the planet which can wander more than sixty km. without coming upon a road and a hundred km. without meeting villages, fields of maize and men.

What we thinks of as wild, virgin Africa is no longer. It is all a huge safari park, like Longleat. Not as tamed, perhaps, not as regulated, certainly not as well run.

Every black and white rhino, every elephant and lion, every shrew and antelope and crocodile and tick-bird and snake and termite is now our responsibility. They will not survive unless we, as the management committee, leave our boardroom tables and act, husband our environment, manage and control and conserve and use it wisely – be that use ploughing it up, driving with video-cameras to eyeball through it, hunting upon it or gazing at it as one might a fine painting.

For if the rhino dies, we die. Perhaps not as quickly, perhaps not as quietly. Yet assuredly we shall, in the end, share the rhino's fate. For every hectare of bush lost to human development another aspect of creation will disappear, another poisoned nail driven into the trunk of the ecological and evolutionary tree. We need the bush and all wild places – and all its wild inhabitants – to maintain the balance of nature upon which all life depends. Without them we are doomed.

We need the rhino and its environment just as much as it needs us for its continued well-being. All life is not a matter of one species dominating another but of mutual co-existence and co-operation under the basic scheme of things. Until this lesson is learned, and taken thoroughly to heart, there can be little hope for any of us, man or beast.

I am reminded of three sentences. The first was spoken by Jim Corbett whose religion was not that of gods in temples but of natural justice: 'The killing of animals without due cause is against all the gods' wills.' The second was spoken by Clement Mwale: 'Which is more important? The man or the animal? It must be the man but he must be responsible for what he is.' The third was spoken by Ron Thomson.

We were standing in the Zambian bush by the skeleton of a black rhino. The bones were sun-bleached and scattered about in the desiccated grass. The skull was badly split where the horn had been axed off. This old bull, which I had seen alive the year before, had been poached during the rainy season. Ron held in his hand one of the animal's rib-bones. His finger was poking through the AK47 bullet hole.

'You know,' he said, quietly, 'I think Africa may have had it.'

For the rhino's sake – and ours – I hope he's very wrong.

Notes and References

PREFACE

1 Dik–dik (*Madoqua kirki*).
2 Thomson's gazelle (*Gazella thomsoni*).

1 RHINO ROAD

1 The tick-bird belongs to the Buphagidae family.

2 THE EVOLUTION OF RHINOS

1 Woolly Rhinoceros (*Coelodonta antiquitatis*).

3 UNICORNS AND OTHER MARVELS

1 Cotton's Rhinoceros (*Ceratotherium simum cottoni*).

4 MOTHER NATURE'S TANK

1 Shrike (*Tchagra tchagra*).

5 THE BLACK RHINO

1 Black rhino (*Diceros bicornis*).
2 Blue rhino (*Rhinoceros keitlos*).
3 Osa Johnson, *I Married Adventure*.
4 Gerenuk (*Litocranius walleri*).
5 Wildebeest (*Connochaertes taurinus*).
6 Topi (*Damaliscus lunatus*).
7 Hartebeest (*Alcelaphus buselaphus*).
8 Filariform worm (*Stephanofilaria dinniki*).
9 Ticks exclusive to the rhino are *Amblyomma rhinocerotis*.
10 White cattle egret (*Bubuleus ibis*).
11 C.A.W. Guggisberg, *Sos Rhino*.

6 THE WHITE RHINO

1 White rhino (*Ceratotherium simum*). *Simum* means 'flat-nosed'.
2 Frederick Courtenay Selous, *A Hunter's Wandering in Africa*.
3 Particularly *Themeda triandra*, the red grass *Urochloa* and the sweet-tasting *Panicum maximum*.

7 IN RHINO COUNTRY

1 John Gordon Davis, *Operation Rhino.*
2 Gilbert Waterhouse, *Simon van der Stal's Journal, and His Expedition to Namaqualand 1685–1686.*
3 William and Irene Morden, *Our African Adventure.*
4 C.A. Spinage, *Animals of East Africa.*
5 George Adamson, *My Pride and Joy.*
6 Capt. C.R.S. Pitman, *A Game Warden Takes Stock.*
7 *East African Standard*, Nairobi, Kenya, 4 May 1926.

8 HUNTERS AND RHINOS

1 Elspeth Huxley, author of *The Flame Trees of Thika* and *The Mottled Lizard*, remarkable autobiographies of childhood in Kenya.
2 Jim Corbett, author of *Man-Eaters of Kumaon, The Temple Tiger, The Man-Eating Leopard of Rudraprayag*, and other books.
3 Quoted from Jan Hemsing, *Ker & Downey Safaris: The Inside Story*
4 George Eastman, *Chronicles of an African Trip.*
5 J.A. Hunter, *Hunter's Tracks.*
6 J.A. Hunter published three books of autobiographical African stories: *Hunter, African Bush Stories*, and *Hunter's Tracks.*
7 Osa Johnson, *Four Years in Paradise.*
8 *Hunter's Tracks.*
9 Bartle Bull, *Safari: A Chronicle of Adventure.*
10 Puka (*Kobus Kob*).
11 Quoted from Mary L. Jobe Akeley, *Carl Akeley's Africa.*

10 THE RHINO AND THE AK47

1 Denis Holman, *The Elephant People.*
2 Scrub olive (*Acokanthera longiflora*).
3 Quoted by Holman.

11 HOW TO CATCH A RHINO

1 *King Solomon's Mines* (1950), directed by Sam Zimbalist. Shot on location in Kenya and Tanganyika, Ruanda-Urundi and Uganda, it starred Stewart Granger and Deborah Kerr.
2 *The Snows of Kilimanjaro*, 20th Century Fox (1952). Directed by Henry King and starring Gregory Peck, Susan Hayward and Ava Gardner.
3 Flaxedil (Gallamine triethiodide).
4 Largactil (Chloropromazine hydrochloride).
5 The active ingredients of Immobilon are etorphine hydrochloride, ace-promazine maleate and chlorocresol.

6 Revivon is a blue solution of diprenorphine, methylene blue and chlorocresol.

7 Such as penimycin or terramycin.

12 GOLDEN HORNS AND OTHER RHINO PARTS

1 The seminal study in this area, without which little would be known of the place of rhino horn in Oriental medicine, exists in *Rhino Exploitation* by Dr Esmond Bradley Martin. I am also indebted to Christopher Hilton for his assistance with information on Chinese medicine.

13 ELECTRIC FENCES, PERSONAL ALARMS AND RHINOS

1 *BBC Wildlife Magazine*, vol. 5, no. 6, June 1987, p.306.

14 LICENSED TO KILL, LICENSED TO CONSERVE

1 Frederick Courtenay Selous, *African Nature Notes and Reminiscences*.

15 DAWN OR DARKNESS

1 Nyala (*Tragelaphus angasi*).

2 W.R. Thomson, *On Wildlife 'Conservation'*.

Bibliography

ADAMSON, GEORGE, *My Pride and Joy* (Collins Harvill 1986)

AKELEY, MARY L. JOBE, *Carl Akeley's Africa* (Dodd, Mead 1929)

BALDWIN, WILLIAM CHARLES, *African Hunting and Adventure* (Bentley 1894)

BEARD, PETER, *The End of the Game* (Chronicle Books 1988)

BULL, BARTLE, *Safari: A Chronicle of Adventure* (Viking 1988)

BURCHELL, WILLIAM, *Selections from Travels in the Interior of Southern Africa* (OUP 1937)

CATTRICK, ALAN, *Spoor of Blood* (Timmins 1959)

CRANWORTH, LORD, *Kenya Chronicles* (Macmillan 1939)

CUMMING, ROUALEYN GORDON, *The Lion Hunter of South Africa* (Murray 1904)

DAVIS, JOHN GORDON, *Operation Rhino* (Michael Joseph 1972)

EASTMAN, GEORGE, *Chronicles of an African Trip* (privately published 1927)

GUGGISBERG, C.A.W., *SOS Rhino* (Andre Deutsch 1966)

HARESNAPE, GEOFFREY, *The Great Hunters* (Purnell 1974)

HARRIS, WILLIAM CORNWALLIS, *The Wild Sports of Southern Africa* (Bohn 1852)

HART, SUSANNE, *Life with Daktari* (Bles 1969)

HEMSING, JAN, *Ker & Downey Safaris: The Inside Story* (Sealpoint 1989)

HOLMAN, DENIS, *The Elephant People* (John Murray 1967)

HUNTER, J.A., *Hunter's Tracks* (Hamish Hamilton 1957)

HUNTER, J.A. & MANNIX, DANIEL, *African Bush Adventures* (Hamilton 1954)

JACKSON, SIR FREDERICK, *Early Days in East Africa* (Arnold 1930)

JOHNSON, OSA, *Four Years in Paradise* (Hutchinson ?)

JOHNSON, OSA, *I Married Adventure* (Lippincott 1940)

KEMP, KENNETH, *Tales of the Big Game Hunters* (Sportsman's Press 1986)

KERNEY, YUILLEEN, *Rufus the Rhino* (Collins 1965)

MARTIN, ESMOND BRADLEY, *Rhino Exploitation* (WWF 1983)

MEINERTZHAGEN, RICHARD, *Kenya Diary* (Eland Books 1983)

MERZ, ANNA, *Rhino: At the Brink of Extinction* (Harper Collins 1991)

MICHAEL, GEORGE, *African Fury* (Michael Joseph 1955)

MILLAIS, J.G., *The Life of Frederick Courtenay Selous* (Longman 1918)

MILLER, CHARLES, *Battle for the Bundu* (Macmillan 1974)

MORDEN, WILLIAM and IRENE, *Our African Adventure* (Seeley, Service 1954)

PERCIVAL, A. BLAYNEY, *A Game Ranger's Notebook* (Nisbet 1925)

PITMAN, C.R.S., *A Game Warden Takes Stock* (Nisbet 1942)

PLAYER, IAN, *The White Rhino Saga* (Collins 1972)

HRH THE PRINCE OF WALES, *Sport and Travel in East Africa* (Allan 1934)

PRINGLE, JOHN, *The Conservationists and the Killers* (Bulpin 1982)

SELOUS, FREDERICK COURTENAY, *African Nature Notes and Reminiscences* (Galagos 1986)

   A Hunter's Wanderings in Africa (Macmillan 1920)

SPINAGE, C.A., *Animals of East Africa* (Collins 1962)

THOMPSON, W.R. (RON), *On Wildlife 'Conservation'* (United Publishers 1986)

TRZEBINSKI, ERROL, *The Kenya Pioneers* (Heinemann 1985)

WATERHOUSE, GILBERT, *Simon van de Stal's Journal, and his Expedition to Namaqualand 1685–1686* (unknown 1932)

Index

Abercrombie and Kent, 115
Aberdare Highlands, 54, 100
Aceratheres, 25
acokanthera, 136–7
Adamson, George, 88, 106, 172
Adamson, Joy, 88, 106
Adow, Sergeant, 122, 123
advertising
    image of rhino in, 142
    to increase public awareness
        about wildlife, 174–5
African rhino *see* Black rhino;
    white rhino
Agatharcides, 32
agricultural encroachment, 52,
    96, 113, 115, 118, 198
AIDS, 198
AK 47 rifles, 122, 125, 131–3,
    166, 167, 202
Akeley, Carl, 116, 195
Algeria, 67
'alicorn', 30, 31
Amynodonts, 25
Animal Ark (television series),
    141
ant-eaters, 44
antelopes, 19, 21, 24, 95, 119,
    156, 161, 180, 189
antibiotics, 150
Anti-Poaching Units (APUs),
    125, 166–7, 168
Antwerp Zoo, 35
aphrodisiac, 156–7, 158
Arabs
    early knowledge about rhino,
        34
    slavers, 182

and trade, 34, 122, 154, 156
and weapon supply, 131, 154
arrows *see* bows and arrows
artiodactyls (even-toed
    ungulates), 24, 28, 39
Aschan, Kris, 97
Asia, 26, 27, 29, 32, 160 *see also*
    names of countries
Athi Plain, 21
Athi river, 187
Australia, 145
azaperone, 148, 149, 150, 151

baboons, 105, 114
Bailey, Mr G.L., 90, 91, 92, 93
Bailey, Mrs, 90–2, 93, 110
Bayreuth, Margrave of, 31
BBC Wildlife Magazine, 170
Bechuanaland, 153, 155
bees, 56
Big Five, 75, 84, 94, 99, 187
bird shoots, 194
black rhino
    breeding, 52, 60–2
    in captivity, 50, 143, 151
    charging, 47, 59–60, 78,
        85–7, 110, 112
    conservation success, 40, 168,
        183
    deaths from, 89–90, 182
    decline in numbers, 52, 53,
        156, 168, 182
    de-horning, 169
    detailed discussion of, 50–62
    difficult to track, 76–7
    dung, 43, 71
    effect of drugs on, 147